through intimacy with God through his Son Jesus Christ. This book will make you hungry for more!

Linda Dulan-Moore
Pastor

I0108934

## About the Cover

The images for both the front and back covers of this book were taken by my daughter, Ginny Smith, as we spent four days at Kentucky's Pine Mountain State Park. I was looking for a path with light at the end to symbolize our progression toward perfection.

The front cover was perfect showing that on our journey there are both light and dark places that we encounter.

But while we were on the trail, I noticed benches spaced periodically and thought how symbolic of the way our Lord gives us places to rest along our way.

Thank you, Ginny, for taking over 200 pictures before we found the perfect two. And thank you, Nick Delliskave, for being an absolutely amazing cover designer.

# *The Progression of Perfection*

Amy Barkman

# Contents

# Introduction

Jesus said, *"Be ye therefore perfect, even as your Father in Heaven is perfect."* (Matthew 5:48) Do you believe that?

Many people say that there is no way we will be perfect until after we die. If that is true, why did Jesus phrase it as a command instead of a promise from God?

In His prayer at the Lord's supper, Jesus prayed not only for His disciples but for those who will believe on Him through their word. He asked God, *"That they all may be one; as thou,*

*Father, art in me, and I in thee, that they also may be one in us: that the world may believe that thou hast sent me*" (John 17:21).

We are one with God? One with Jesus? How is the world going to believe in Jesus through our oneness with Him and the Father if our perfection isn't going to happen until heaven?

John also writes, "*He that saith he abideth in Him ought himself also so to walk, even as He walked*" (I John 2:6). If we say we live in Jesus Christ, we are to walk like Him. Hmm, multiplying food for the hungry, healing the sick, casting out demons, raising the dead, walking on water, living a completely pure and obedient life?

How did Jesus and John expect people like you and me to be perfect, complete in moral character, to be one with Jesus and the Father, to walk like Jesus walked? Many of us don't believe that's even possible. Is it any wonder so much of the Church has put off that perfection until heaven?

Those who believe that perfection isn't attainable in this life are wrong. Scripture tells us Jesus is coming for a *perfect* Church. "*That he might present it to himself a glorious church, not having spot, or wrinkle, or any such thing; but that it should be holy and without blemish.*" (Ephesians 5:27) Another proof of His design for us is in Revelation 19:7 "*Let us be glad and rejoice and give honour to Him: for the marriage of the Lamb is come, and His wife hath made her-self ready."*

We, the bride of Christ, the church, are not going to be made instantly perfect – except physically - at the coming of Jesus, we are to make ourselves ready for that coming!

If that is true - and we who believe Scripture know it is - then how can we get there?

Several years ago, the Lord started dealing with me on that very topic. I realized that perfection is our goal, but it doesn't happen overnight. There is definitely a journey and process to perfection, a progression of increasing holiness.

Everything along the path of our progression to the perfection God wants for us can be seen in three parts. Each part consists of many steps. Those parts are:

1. Make Jesus your Lord.
2. Make Jesus your Love.
3. Make Jesus your Life.

In this book we will examine these parts and their steps. I pray that each of us progresses in our journey as easily and quickly as possible. At the end of the book, there is a Reflections section for each chapter, questions for you to ask yourself about your progression to perfection. You can use them after each chapter or save them to do all together when you finish the book. I hope they help you see yourself on the map of your journey.

When I started this book, I had no idea of how much of my own story I was going to include but the Lord kept bringing illustrations to mind. Some of them would be kind of embarrassing if I hadn't been delivered from caring what people think. I hope my experiences help you recall or have your own times of being set free.

And I want to explain why I use the King James Version in my quotes. There are people who believe that it is the only accurate translation; I don't believe that, but I want this book to reach everyone. I believe God's Word is true in any translation, because it is *living* and speaks to our spirits in addition to our minds.

# PART ONE

# LORD

# Chapter One
# Recognize your Need for a Savior

"I think that stuff is all ridiculous. A loving God would never send people to hell or send his son to suffer all that torture. It's just a stupid belief."

Actually I changed the wording – drastically. The original statement did not include "stuff," "ridiculous," or "stupid belief," but were profanities. My friend had been turned off by Christian leaders in his high school years and in college and became an atheist. Though I very much disliked his hatred and his vocabulary, I understood his anger. But as I told him, if Christianity is "ridiculous" I am ridiculous and so is my whole life.

When I told him that God loves him, he asked if God loved Adolph Hitler. I replied yes, God loved Hitler but didn't like his actions. Then I posted that question on Facebook and got the answer, "Yes God loved Adolph Hitler" from the majority of my Christian friends. When I reported the survey, my atheist friend said, "Christians are weird." It occurred to me that his definition of love is affection where God's definition of love is active good will, grace, mercy, and the desire for relationship.

This man is one of five atheists I know personally and care about deeply, and the only one I've discussed Christianity with to any depth, but I began to see something.

The first step to becoming a Christian is to know your need for a Savior. God loves us "just as we are" but I don't always like myself just as I am. I have many imperfections. When I first came to that realization, I knew I needed help. And I still do!

The word "sin" essentially means "missing the mark." And what is the mark? Perfection, being in the image of God. And we humans really miss the mark of perfection. Yet we are commanded to have no other gods before Him (Exodus 20:3), to love Him with all our heart, soul, strength, and mind (Matthew 22:37), and to be perfect even as He is perfect (Matthew 5:48).

Obviously none of us can reach these goals on our own. We need help! We need someone who can get rid of our imperfections. We need someone who can help us become what we were created to be.

And there is only One who can do that: God.

The triune nature of God is confusing to people, even Christians. There is God the Father, God the Son, and God the Holy Spirit. God the Father is known as the Creator of all that exists (well, He is known as the Creator by those who believe that all which exists was created instead of just magically evolving from something).

I've studied quantum physics a little over the past 20 years and believe that the "Big Bang" was when God said, "LIGHT BE!" Actually, the first three verses of the Bible identify the entire trinity as being present and having a part in creation.

Genesis 1: 1 *In the beginning God created the heaven and the earth. 2. And the earth was without form and void; and darkness was upon the face of the deep. And the Spirit of God moved upon the face of the waters. 3. And God said, "Let there be light": and there was light.*

1. The Father created atoms 2. The Holy Spirit hovered over them (made waves) 3. And the Son (the Word of God) spoke as to how those

atoms were to come together. All things are created with light and sound waves. There are more wave possibilities than physical particles in our bodies and in everything around us.

When I teach on "Quantum Physics and the Bible," I always mention Shadrach, Meshach and Abednigo. They (along with Daniel) were *"children in whom was no blemish, but well favoured, and skillful in all wisdom, and cunning in knowledge, and understanding science, and such as had ability in them to stand in the king's palace..."* (Daniel 1:4).

When you become a Christian, you spiritually have no blemish, and are well favored by God. Jesus is made unto you wisdom (1 Corinthians 1:30.) You can be still and know the Lord as well as receive knowledge from the Holy Spirit. And you can stand before THE KING, God Himself. Did you see the part I skipped – understanding science? How do you think those three men could emerge from an extremely hot furnace and come out without a burn and not even smelling like smoke? They not only trusted God, we are told they understood science. They understood His creation, the science of things, as did Daniel who was not hurt in the den of lions.

Okay, I promise I'm through with talking about science, at least for now. Science is the way things really work in this physical world, and I hope you can see that the more you learn about creation, the easier it is to have faith in God's miraculous ability, not only to create but to change things. He created the way this world works, and He operates the way He created it to work.

Now back to our nature. Why did God make us this way? The answer to that question is: *He didn't!*

When God created everything, including humans, He made all perfect. And He gave authority over all created things to the humans. They could have and do anything they chose – except one thing.

No. Forget about eating apples.

The word tree used in the Bible about the Tree of Knowledge of Good and Evil in the Garden of Eden basically means in the Hebrew/Aramaic firmness. It comes from a root word which means firm or to shut. Think about it. This implies permanence – something set, solid, and not open to change. The fruit of that tree would cause a permanent change in those who partook of it.

What God was saying to Adam was "Take of everything I've created but there is one thing that I do not want you to partake of: permanently knowing both good and evil. If you make that part of your nature, you will die to My nature which I put in you – love and goodness." But they ate of that tree anyway. Eve did it because she was deceived and Adam because he chose to be one with Eve instead of God and what He had told him before Eve was even created. This is why it is called 'Adam's sin'. He knew what he was doing. She didn't.

When they did partake of the fruit that changed their nature, God put Adam and his wife out of the garden so that they could not eat of the Tree of Life and remain forever in that fallen condition.

But because they partook of the knowledge of good and evil and it became part of them, that nature was in their genes and DNA, and was passed down to all their descendants. Including you and me.

That is sad. God was sad about it. And you and I are sad about it. But it is a fact.

Our very nature now is to be one with both good and evil. There is no separate human nature; there is the nature of God and the nature of the devil. Human nature is the ability to choose which nature we act on at given times. And because of the generations that have added to our genetic inheritance, we often cannot choose good; we are born with addictions that we have no control over. Those addictions can be physical or emotional. And I wonder since Eve, who was deceived, was the mother of all, as Adam named her, could this be why we are so easily deceived?

I know many people who have inherited an addiction, or constant need for, alcohol. I personally, because of two generations that I know about, inherited a fascination with and need for romance. That particular addiction was encouraged by growing up in the age of movies like *Cinderella* and *Singing in the Rain*.

The Word of God tells us Jesus was tempted in every area which we are, but He never sinned. He chose the nature of God every time He had a choice. (Hebrews 4:15) Can you even imagine that? Jesus was tempted by alcohol, pride, gossip, sex, theft, hatred, violence and on and on. I can't imagine it. But it's true. He spent His life choosing to walk in God's Love and Holiness.

We will talk about love and holiness later but right now I just wanted to make sure we understand why we need a Savior. And amazing above amazing, God chose to send a part of Himself to be that Savior, a human, the Word of God made flesh, the second Adam (I Corinthians 15:45), who chose correctly to be one with only good, not evil; who chose to take upon Himself the consequences of our rebellion: pain, sorrow, and suffering beyond our imaginations, who chose to offer us a new life.

# Chapter Two
# Receive Forgiveness and Rebirth

Now that we have seen the basis of our need of a Savior and the reality of our inability to be perfect, we will talk about what we are to do to let that Savior save us.

The Gospel, or the Good News, is that Jesus – whose name in Hebrew is Yeshua, which means Salvation – came from God, to restore what was lost in the fall of mankind in the Garden of Eden. He did and does several things.

1. He was born as a human and experienced everything humans experience, except sin,

although He experienced sinful desires and the temptation to sin. (Heb. 4:15).

2. He demonstrated the nature of His Father in all that He did: forgiving, healing, providing, showing us what a human child of God should be like. (John 14:9)

3. He received our sins in His own body and then took them to the cross on Calvary and experienced the deserved punishment for every evil ever committed. He died spiritually, soulishly, and physically in our place.

4. He rose from the dead with new life – for Himself and all who will receive what He did for them.

5. He sent the Holy Spirit, the power part of God, to all mankind so they can receive from God.

Does all that convince you that the Almighty loves you? I hope so.

So the first thing we do is accept the truth about who Jesus is and what He did.

The second thing we do is receive the forgiveness that He died to give us.

The third thing we do is invite Him to live in us and give us new life.

Like my friend who believes that Christianity is a bunch of "ridiculousness," many find it difficult to accept the truth about who Jesus is, especially when we see so much ungodliness out of those who claim to be His followers. Not only are there sinful acts there is pride and misunderstanding of truth.

When a person receives new life, they are not new throughout their minds, emotions, will, or bodies. What happens is they receive the life of God in their spirit – their new life. Then they begin a process of working that new life outwards, or that is what they are supposed to do! The term 'born again' comes from Jesus Himself in the third chapter of the book of John, *"Truly I say to you that except a man be born again, he cannot see the kingdom of God."* When questioned by Nicodemus who was searching for truth, Jesus went on to say the most well-known sentence in the whole New Testament, *"For God so loved the world that he gave his only begotten Son, that whosoever believeth in him should not perish but have everlasting life."* (John 3:16) And I love what came after that. Jesus said that the Father didn't send His son into the world to condemn it but to save it, that the world is already condemned; but those who receive the light, the truth which is Jesus, will be saved.

At one point in that discussion, Jesus said, *"Except a man be born of water and of the Spirit, he cannot enter into the kingdom of God."* A lot of people believe that means water baptism. Although I believe in water baptism, I personally think He meant the water of the Word. We are born again by the living Word empowered by the

Holy Spirit.

But in order to do that, in order to receive that new life, we must receive forgiveness. And that's not always easy. I have met many, many people who are so overwhelmed by guilt and feel so unworthy that they cannot receive a Savior. Our job as believers in Jesus Christ is to show them how much God loves them and had Jesus pay for their sins.

Years ago I had a neighbor named Janie. She came to church every Sunday, but she had not accepted Jesus. When I questioned her, she said it was because she was not worthy, she had too many sins. When I tried to explain about how Jesus took the punishment for those sins, she just shook her head. I prayed and prayed and said everything I could think of. This went on for over a year, and every Sunday I watched from the choir as Janie clutched the pew in front of her when the invitation was given, and the invitation hymn was played. And often she wept, but she never answered that invitation. One Sunday morning Janie was weeping more than usual, and I heard the Lord say to me, "Cry with Janie." What? If I did that, the congregation might think I had done some sin! Then it hit me – that was pride, so I obeyed the Lord. I let the pain and anguish that was the Holy Spirit's desire for her come out in great demonstration of weeping. Within ten seconds, Janie let go of the pew and came forward to receive forgiveness and new life from her Lord.

We will be looking at forgiveness more later, but it is so important to receive it as the second step to a new life. Don't ever let pride keep you from receiving forgiveness, or from helping someone else receive.

## Read The Word

The way we know these things are true about Jesus is because of the Bible, the written word that God gave to everyone through His chosen scribes. This word is about Himself and His actions. It is primarily about His love for us. Frankly the more I read the Bible I am amazed at His patience and grace and mercy.

By the way, grace is when we get what we don't deserve, and mercy is when we don't get what we do deserve! I love that definition of mercy. It always makes me smile. I have received a lot of mercy. Haven't you?

The part of the Bible called the New Testament means New Covenant. The Old Covenant was made with the Hebrew people, and the New Covenant was between the Father and Son. It includes all who accept Him as their Savior. The New Testament is the part of the Bible where Jesus comes and we see how He lived. After that, we see how He died, for us! And then we see how He was raised from the dead and gave life to all who believe. Later we see how His disciples went out to tell everyone what He did and show that His power still works through them. Then there are letters to those who were alive at that time and to those who will be believers down through the ages...all the way to you and me. Those letters teach us what God wants to do in our lives.

I suggest that new Christians (a Christian is a part of the Body of Christ – someone who believes Jesus died for their sins and was raised from the dead to give new life to them), read the New Testament first. Then when you read the Old Testament, or Old Covenant, you can see how from the beginning God loved us and planned to win us back from this evil world.

Much of the Old Testament is a dress rehearsal for the New Testament. From the beginning, God was getting His people to accept His ways.

Why?

Because when God created mankind, He gave them authority over everything in the earth. He never took back that authority, so over and over He asked mankind to agree to things that He then would bring about to save us all.

One of the greatest examples is when Abraham agreed to sacrifice his son at God's command. But before he could complete that sacrifice, God provided a ram for him to sacrifice instead. But that gave the authority to God to sacrifice His son as a replacement for man's sin.

Another example is when the Hebrew nation were slaves in Egypt. God told them to each take a lamb into their homes for several days. Then they were to kill it and put its blood on their door, and when the angel of death, that went through and killed all the firstborn of Egypt, saw that blood, he would pass over their home.

God provided a sacrifice, and the blood of Jesus causes the angel of death to pass over us. But because man had authority in the earth, man first obeyed and agreed to The Plan, although they didn't know it was a much larger plan than they were experiencing.

When we obey the Lord and read the Bible we find out many things about His Love and His Plan to buy us back from the devil to whom we gave ourselves, our souls, our minds, emotions, and wills.

We read earlier that the Lord sends His Spirit to live in us. It is that Spirit who makes the written Word come alive to us. If we don't have the Holy Spirit working in us, the Bible does not make sense. When I was young, I had a Sunday School teacher tell me that the Bible is a good book and has a lot of wisdom in it, but you can't take it literally. It was nearly twenty years later that I discovered the truth – that the Bible is the living Word of God which, when believed, changes you. There are parts of the Word which are illustrations and not facts, but they are still Truth.

In Mark 4:33-34, we learn that Jesus spoke the Word in parables (a story designed to teach a truth) to the people and didn't speak any other way to them because they wouldn't be able to understand it.

Let's look at one of these parables about the Word of God. In Mark 4:3-8, Jesus told a story about someone who went out to sow some seed. Some fell away from the field and were immediately devoured by the fowls of the air. Some fell on the ground, but it was filled with stones, and though the seed sprang up, it had no roots and was killed by the heat of the sun. Some fell on the ground among thorns which choked out any growth of fruit. But some fell on good ground and was healthy and grew and brought forth much fruit.

Then Jesus explained – in Mark 4:13-30 – that the seed is the Word of God. He said the seed that fell away from the field is that which Satan comes immediately to take out of the hearts of those in whom it was sown. The ones who had the Word sown but had no root of faith in God were at first glad but then when something bad happens, they give up believing it. The ones who have the seed sown among thorns represent those who hear the word, but their own temptations and desires choke the word and it can't work in or for them. The ones who receive the word in their hearts and believe it bring forth fruit in differing amounts.

A very interesting thing is that Jesus says before His explanation in Mark 4:14: *"If you don't understand this parable, you won't understand any parable."* Wow! The Word of God, the seed sown in your heart, is the most important thing in all the world, to help you know Him and grow up into who He created you to be. We can't understand anything without understanding the importance of the Word of God sown in our hearts and minds.

Read it, listen to it. Input that Word in every way you can.

## Chapter Three
## Receive the Holy Spirit

Genesis 1: 1 *In the beginning God created the heaven and the earth. 2. And the earth was without form and void; and darkness was upon the face of the deep. And the Spirit of God moved upon the face of the waters. 3. And God said, "Let there be light": and there was light.*

Even for Christians, the Holy Spirit is probably the most misunderstood part of our God. I had an experience over 50 years ago that I love to share.

I was in an abusive marriage and had started

back to church. One day when my children were at their grandmother's and my husband was working, I was home alone reading my Bible when I came across a verse: "*Let nothing be done through strife or vainglory; but in lowliness of mind let each esteem other better than themselves.*" Philippians 2:3. I set my Bible down in a state of shock. I went to the phone and called my pastor. "How can I esteem my husband better than myself when I wouldn't treat an insect the way he treats me?"

My pastor said, "Do you pray?" I started to answer, "Yes," and then had a picture of my six-year-old self kneeling beside my bed passionately seeking God. I answered, "No, I think thoughts toward God, but don't really pray." He said, "Go do that."

I hung up and went to the living room and knelt in front of the couch. I immediately saw a picture of a motion picture projector and heard these words – in my head, not out loud. "Humans are like a motion picture projector. They either give forth evil things or good things according to their choices." And I felt as though a warm blanket had been thrown around my shoulders and body. I knew it was the Lord. Then after a couple of minutes, His Presence faded away and I was left in a state of shock. I got up, lit a cigarette, and fixed a bourbon and coke to calm my trembling body. (Go ahead and shake your head. I do every time I think about it. By the way, I quit drinking over thirty years ago and quit smoking twenty-seven years ago.)

The next morning I was in the choir at church and time came for the "Moments of Meditation" where the pastor had the church be silent for sixty seconds. I asked God for forgiveness for the smoking and drinking in reaction to experiencing His actual presence the day before. Immediately something happened. I don't know whether I was in the body or out but the church building, and congregation were nowhere to be seen. I was in the presence of a man-shaped body of light who loved me beyond measure and felt humor at my situation. He communicated to me, "You need to learn to love. When you learn to love, those things you consider big, bad sins will melt away as though they never were."

Then I was back, aware of the church and the pastor speaking again.

I knew it only lasted sixty seconds, but it seemed as though I had spent eternity in that loving Presence. And then "learn to love?" I had gone to God in the first place because I thought I was so loving, and my husband wasn't. Wow! Obviously I had a lot to learn.

There was never a time when I thought I made that up but there were a lot of times in the beginning when the scripture that says the devil appears as an angel of light (II Cor. 11:14) came to my mind and the enemy tried to convince me that it was him, not God who appeared to me. One of the things that helped me fight that lie was because that afternoon my Daddy called me and asked, "Did you scrub your face extremely hard this morning?" I was shocked but answered, "No, sir. Why?" He said, "One time when I looked up at you in the choir, your face was shining very brightly." I thought of Moses who had to cover his face after being in the presence of the Lord because of the light that hurt the eyes of the people. I thanked the Lord for that confirmation.

After I resolved that it truly was God that I saw and heard, I tried to define what part of Himself. It was man-shaped so was it Jesus? That didn't feel right. But then the Father didn't feel right either.

It was twenty two years later when I was reading Benny Hinn's book *Good Morning, Holy Spirit* that I put the book down and said, very uncomfortably, "Holy Spirit, it seems strange to talk to you. I talk to the Father and Jesus, but I don't really know you except as a power that sometimes works through me to help others. Can you make yourself better known to me?" Immediately my mind flashed back twenty-two years to that time in the choir loft with the Person who loved me beyond my comprehension and was amused at my confusion. Then I heard,

"That was me!" That was Him? The Holy Spirit manifest where I could see and hear Him? He who always holds up Jesus and not Himself. I began weeping with love, and amazement at His humility – and I cried off and on for two days.

I try not to be judgmental when people say the Holy Spirit is a dove. And I know that the dove and the flame are symbols of Him, but He is a person. Anne Graham Lotz recently wrote a book called *Jesus in Me: Experiencing the Holy Spirit as a Constant Companion* about the Holy Spirit , and in the opening she said what I just said and have said for years – He is not a dove or a flame but a person. They are symbols but not Himself. When I read that in her book, I wept again, with joy of confirmation.

I have an enemy and you have an enemy who wants to take out every Word of God from our hearts and minds. He wants to convince us that we never hear God and that we make up things we want to believe. But he is the father of lies (John 8:44). You keep seeking God's confirmation and you will receive it!

Another thing about the Holy Spirit that Christians disagree about are the Gifts of the Spirit. When the Holy Spirit comes, He, as in the second verse of Genesis, is hovering over you waiting to empower the Word in you. In the next chapter, we will look at the Gifts of the Spirit.

# Chapter Four
# Gifts of the Spirit

There are Christians who believe that all the power gifts passed away with the last apostle. There are Christians who believe that you haven't been immersed in the Holy Spirit unless you speak with other tongues. There are Christians who believe all kinds of things in between. I personally received the gifts of Word of Wisdom, Word of Knowledge, and Prophecy decades before I received the gift of Tongues.

The gifts of the Spirit as listed in I Corinthians 12 are: Word of Wisdom, Word of

Knowledge, Faith, Healings, Working of Miracles, Prophecy, Discerning of Spirits, Tongues, and Interpretation of Tongues. I'd like to describe them as I believe they are manifested.

A Word of Wisdom is a Word from God about how to handle a situation or what to do in the future. A Word of Knowledge is a Word from God about something the person receiving needs to understand. The Gift of Faith is a surety beyond the ordinary faith which we all receive that something God promised is going to happen. The Gifts of Healing can be a healing of physical ailments, inner healing, or relational healing. Working of Miracles goes beyond healing to replacement of something missing in the body, or provision that looks like it couldn't happen, or other things that seem to be impossible. Prophecy can be foretelling of future events but usually it is a Word from God to edify and comfort the one prophesied to. Discerning of Spirits is to see into the spirit realm and perceive if a person has a good spirit or is being tormented by evil spirits. Tongues is to speak in a language unknown to the speaker or usually to any human, though sometimes it is used to speak to people of different nations. Interpretation of Tongues is to understand what is being said in that unknown language, if it is not your native tongue being spoken.

I will share a few stories about my

experiences with the Gifts of the Spirit. I am a member of the American Association of Christian Counselors, as a pastor, not a licensed counselor. I don't get paid for counseling. I realized that is a calling because I "just know" sometimes during counseling what will help the person in the situation they are having problems with – that is a Word of Wisdom.

One of the most dramatic gifts I ever received was when one night I visited, for the first and only time, a particular Pentecostal church. I realized later that even the inner push to go was a Word of Knowledge that I was supposed to be there. A man I'll refer to as Greg went up to receive the baptism (immersion) of the Holy Spirit and everyone went up and gathered round him and loudly prayed and cast out a spirit of alcoholism but the man didn't seem to receive, especially the speaking in tongues they expected. But the Lord was revealing things to me. I knew who the man was because he had worked for my husband several times, but I didn't really know him. After the service, I asked if I could talk to him and he agreed so we went over and stood alone by a window. I said, "The Lord told me that something happened to you when you were six years old that is keeping you from receiving from the Holy Spirit. You need to get alone with the Lord and let Him heal that, and you will receive." He just nodded. I knew that what had happened was sexual molestation but didn't want to embarrass him by naming it. The next afternoon when my husband came home from work, he said, "I ran into Greg today and he said 'Last night at church your wife told me something that nobody on earth knew about, not even my parents, only God." We moved away shortly after that and two years later when we moved back, that man was not only freed from alcohol and had received the Holy Spirit. He had become an evangelist.

The Gift of Faith has happened to me a few times but not often. I have been used in the Gift of physical Healing several times. I've noticed that it usually happens when the person needing healing believes that God uses me in that way. There was one lady, a church janitor, who received immediately every time I prayed for her physical healing. But that's not true for everyone. Most of the time I am used for inner healing.

Only twice that I know of have I been used with the Gift of Miracles – and those for myself. One day when I worked for the State of Kentucky I was driving home on an icy road and my car started sliding off the road, right toward a drop off of about thirty feet. I pumped the brake, nothing. Just when I was a few feet from going over the edge, I thought about the promises of protection in Psalm 91 and I couldn't think of words but I shook my head and said, "Uh, uh" meaning, "this can't happen." Immediately without my touching the brake or anything, the car stopped moving. I turned it around and drove home without a further incident.

The other time was when I had just fixed Sunday dinner after church for my family of seven. I was concerned about my creamed corn which everyone loves because I had only had six ears. Then the doorbell rang and there was another family of seven, my husband's relatives. Oh no! They were from out of town and had not eaten after church. I knew I could give each person one piece of chicken instead of two and spread the green beans and mashed potatoes around. There would be enough rolls and dessert for everyone. But the corn! As the family visited with each other and I finished cooking, I stirred the corn and prayed, "Please Lord, multiply this corn." I don't know how it happened but all fourteen of us had corn. I had two helpings and there was some left over. Even with just my seven there had never before been any corn left over!

Sometimes the Lord uses the Gift of Prophecy to tell the future but usually it is exactly what I Cor. 14 says it is – to edify and comfort. That happens through many in the Body of Christ. And I personally, after being a pastor for over 21 years, believe it is a pastoral calling.

I have been given Discerning of Spirits many times when I don't want it. When I sense something negative about anybody I think I am being judgmental, which is my greatest fear. But nearly always it turns out to be a discerning of an evil spirit. And one time I walked into a room at my work, a part of the building where I didn't know anyone. And I knew that there was not a single Christian in that room of about a dozen people.

I'd like to add something here about evil spirits. If you look up the words in the original Greek, the word evil means destructive and the word spirit means life form. Think about that...a destructive life form. That can be anything from drug addiction to anger or sorrow issues to cancer. It is something that comes originally from the hater of mankind, the enemy, the devil. Jesus said *"The thief comes only to kill, steal, and destroy. I have come that they may have life and have it in abundance."* (John 10:10)

If it is a destructive life form, it is NOT from God.

My favorite story about discernment of spirits, however, is very different. A friend of mine wanted me to go with her to the hospital to pray for her landlady who she said was a very difficult non-Christian woman. The woman was dying, and Diane wanted her to know about Jesus so she could go to heaven. I agreed and as soon as we walked in the hospital room and I looked at the lady, I knew. After Diane introduced us, I went over to the bed and touched her shoulder. "When were you baptized?" Immediately a beautiful smile lit up her face. She answered by describing the wonderful time of being baptized in the river and into Jesus, her Savior. I could see out of the corner of my eye that my friend had almost fallen against the wall and was holding her heart in shock!

And now the most divisive of the gifts – Tongues. According to what I've heard, the Gift of Tongues can be someone speaking in a human language they don't know to those who use that language. It can be speaking in the language of angels. It can be speaking in an individual language unknown to anyone. But it is the Holy Spirit giving the words that are needed by a recipient. I never wanted to speak in tongues publicly, but I do pray in tongues and when I do, sometimes I see in my mind people that I am praying for according to God's will. Once I saw a man on the sidewalk in New York City with much traffic going down the street. Once I saw a nun kneeling in a convent in France. I saw them and knew the Spirit was having me pray for them, but I didn't know what their needs or my prayers were. My prayer partner, Jacque, was praying in tongues once and saw a teenage girl wracked with agony from an overdose of drugs. We are told the Holy Spirit *"makes intercession for the saints according to the will of God."* Romans 8:27

But Interpretation of Tongues is another matter. For some reason, the Holy Spirit uses me in this gift a lot. Nearly always if I am in a church or gathering where someone gives a message in tongues, I know what is said – and know when I am to give the interpretation.

My most vivid memory is my first visit to the national conference which is the full gospel part of the United Methodist Church, Aldersgate Renewal Ministries. I went for the preparatory two days before the conference started and was taught that no one was to give a word of any kind without checking with the Spiritual Direction team. The opening night a man who either didn't go to the classes or just disobeyed the rule, got up and gave a long and loud message in tongues. I immediately knew what the Lord was saying but I didn't want to go up before thousands of people and give it. There was silence. And more silence. I thought surely these people who were more spiritual than I was, and who had been to ARM before would get the interpretation. More silence. Finally, the man who was the head of the organization got up in front of the crowd and said, "For this to be scriptural, someone has the interpretation. Please come forward." I started up front and thought, "Now I know what the expression means 'feeling like a lamb led to slaughter'." When I reached the front, I looked over at the team questioningly. They all nodded almost violently. I don't remember what that word was, but I found out later that there were over twenty Baptists from up north somewhere who came to the Conference. They had been studying the Holy Spirit and wanted to know more. They didn't trust the Pentecostals but thought maybe they could trust Spirit filled Methodists, which I found amusing. That night after the meeting, every one of them received the Holy Spirit along with speaking in other tongues. The next afternoon one of the Baptist ladies stopped me in the hall and asked, "Why was the man's message in tongues so long and your message was much shorter?" I replied, "Because it isn't a translation; it's an interpretation of what God is pouring out." And she understood.

Another memorable Interpretation experience happened shortly after I received that gift. I was a member of an interdenominational full gospel church, and a woman gave a message in tongues. I immediately saw a vision of Jesus in front of the congregation dressed in armor. I was thinking about what should be said – *I am the Lord your helper, Protector*? Then I thought it was such a masculine thing that a man should interpret it. Shortly after that a man said in a very strong voice, "I AM the Lord your Defender!" Perfect. I knew what God was telling us, but the man said it better than I would have.

The gifts of the Spirit are for the receiver; gifts from God to someone who needs that gift from Him. We, the Body of the Anointed One, are the packages through which the gifts are given. But we have to allow ourselves to be filled.

The Holy Spirit is a wonderful amazing person. We will look at the fruits of the Spirit later.

# Chapter Five
# Obey and Commune

We are to read the Word of God, the scriptures, the Bible. And we are also to obey that Word. I talked about the Holy Spirit before talking about being obedient to the Lord, because without the Holy Spirit it is impossible for us to obey. We'll talk more in depth about Him later.

The main commandment is, *"Love the Lord your God with all your heart and soul and strength and mind."* (Mark 12:30) But think about it for just a minute. Can you imagine doing that – loving someone you've never seen or heard more than your parents, children, spouse, siblings, friends, romantic partner? No matter what you've heard about Him dying for you, you can appreciate Him but love Him more than any other?

But let's pass that by for the time being and think about some other obedience issues. We are not to steal. That means everything from taking a candy bar from Walmart to cheating on your income tax. Have you ever sold something without being honest with the buyer about its true condition? Have you ever turned in more hours of work to get paid for than you actually spent working? When you were in school, did you ever copy someone's homework?

Have you ever born false witness – which means to lie? Interestingly enough, if you have done some of the things we mentioned about stealing, you have also lied. Cheating on your income tax, not being honest about something you sold, turning in more hours than you worked, saying the homework was your own work – all these things involve lying as well as stealing. I grew up with an FBI agent father whose opinion was that lying was the worst thing you could ever do and we kids knew that if we lied we would go straight to hell. So I became an expert at not lying. But also, an expert at deception. One example comes to mind. "Mother, my friends are going bowling Saturday night. May I go out too?" "Of course," she said. So I went out, not with my friends but to the movie. You see? No lie. I didn't say I was going out with them, just stated the truth about my friends and asked if I could go out Saturday night also. You'll laugh when you hear the movie that I was so deceptive about. No, it wasn't something crude or racy. It was Charlton Heston's *The Ten Commandments*. I'd already seen it four times in the two weeks it was in my hometown and my parents were concerned about me becoming a religious fanatic, so they would not agree for me to see it again. So I broke one of the Ten Commandments so I could see it again. By the way I am still good at deception without lying. But I now have my own version of *The Ten Commandments* that I can watch whenever I want. I've finally accepted the fact that deception without lying is still "bearing false witness." That was hard to give up! I've repented a lot!

It's the same kind of thing about not committing adultery. Many of us can say with pride that we have never committed adultery, meaning we have never had intercourse with someone when we were married to another person. But Jesus really messes up that pride thing too. *"You have heard that it was said by them of old time, Thou shalt not commit adultery. But I say unto you, that whosoever looketh on a woman to lust after her hath committed adultery with her already in his heart.*" (Matthew 27,28). Oh dear, I don't think he just meant that for males. I think it applies to everyone. And the word lust used by Him is not just having sexual passion for someone. The word in the Greek is *epithymeo* and means "to set the heart upon, long for, covet, desire' and the last English translation is "lust after." Hmmm. Has anyone who feels pride for not committing a physical act ever longed for or set their heart upon someone who is not their spouse, or who is someone else's spouse? I know very few women who have not at some time done that. I don't know about men; they don't tell me their inner problems about romance and sex as much as women do.

And then there is murder. I've never murdered anyone – good for me! But Jesus said, "*You have heard that it was said by them of old time 'Thou shalt not kill; and whosoever shall kill shall be in danger of the judgment'. But I say to you that whosoever is angry with his brother without a cause shall be in danger of the judgment: and whosoever shall say to his brother 'Raca' (Greek Rhaka: worthless) shall be in danger of the council: but whosoever shall say 'Thou fool' (Greek – moros: stupid, blockhead, absurd, fool) shall be in danger of hell fire.*" (Matthew 5:21,22) Whew! I never felt angry with someone without cause and I never called anyone worthless or stupid. At least not to their face. But what if it's like the adultery thing? What if thinking it, or, let's be honest, saying it about them to someone else, is the same sin? Thank God for the forgiveness that saves me from the danger of hell fire.

Jesus also said something else very difficult to obey. *"I say to you, love your enemies, bless them that curse you, do good to them that hate you, and pray for them which despitefully use you and persecute you."* And He then He continues, *"That you may be the children of your Father which is in heaven; for He makes His sun to rise on the evil and on the good, and sends rain on the just and on the unjust."* (Matthew 5:44,45) We'll be looking more closely at this also in Part Two but think about it? Do you love your enemies? Thank God that the word for love Jesus used is not *phileo* which means 'be fond of' and 'have personal attachment', but the word in Greek here is *agapeo* which means 'love in a social or moral sense.' Isn't that a relief?

You may have noticed that I often explain the original Hebrew or Greek meanings of words. That is because in my desire to obey the Word of God, I want to know exactly what was said. That is why I have – don't laugh – a *Strong's Exhaustive Concordance of the Bible*, which includes both the Hebrew and Greek dictionaries, in my library, my living room, my bedroom, my parlor, and at church. I also have the *Brown, Driver, Briggs Hebrew and English Lexicon*, the *Theological Wordbooks of the Old and New Testaments*, and the four volume *Interpreter's Dictionary of the Bible*. And a few others also, along with many interpretations of the Bible. The versions I use most are the King James, New International Version, and New King James. I use the King James version most because it is the one that is referenced in Strong's Concordance.

The last thing we'll discuss in this first part of our Progression – Making Him our Lord – is about communing with Him. I believe this is one of the most important, and most ignored, steps in our journey. And definitely Communing with Him leads to Part Two, making Him our Love.

You may recall my story about the pastor asking me if I prayed and I started to say yes but remembered the first time I truly communed with the Lord, and honestly answered, "No." The first time I communed with Him, He put His life in me. The second time I communed with Him, He sent the Holy Spirit to me. Wow! I'll probably tell a lot more stories before this book ends! I have been very blessed by communion with Him, probably because I desperately sought it.

I have a wall hanging in my bedroom that I see the first thing when I wake up and the last thing when I turn out my light at night. It is the first part of Psalm 46:10: "Be still and know that

I Am God." In the Hebrew, these words mean: still- *rapa*: cease, forsake, leave alone, and others; Know – *yad*: come with open hands, fellowship, with me and others; God –*Elohim*: God plural, very great and mighty.

When I see that, I feel Him telling me to cease worrying, draw toward Him, forsake other thoughts, leave the future alone, and come to Him with open hands to fellowship and receive and spend time with Him that I may know Him-Father , Son, and Holy Spirit- and that He is very great and mighty and can handle all of my problems.

He wants you to experience that wonderful communion also. He loves you beyond comprehension.

There was one time when for one second I had a recognition of Him as Three in One, but it was quickly gone and I can't even describe it, except for that one second I understood. Most of the time my communion has been with the Father, Son, or Holy Spirit instead of the three in one.

One of my favorite communion times with Him takes some background explaining. When I was sixteen I got pregnant. My parents, who were very concerned about what people thought and very socially minded, wanted me to get an abortion which was illegal at the time. My Daddy was an FBI agent but that is how important it was to them to keep the family away from scandal. I refused. Probably the first time in my life I refused anything. I ended up marrying the child's father and dropped out of high school and went with him to his college and took my first college course during the semester I was pregnant. That summer I had a little girl and she was named after her father's mother, Virginia, and my great-grandmother, Ellen. She grew up to be an amazing person, volunteers to feed the poor, sang with a gospel group, made a hymn CD of her own, and has now written almost forty Christian novels. One day I was in my parlor praying and asked Him, "Lord, did you mean for me to sin? Ginny is one of the most wonderful people, helping the poor and hungry, helping other writers, writing to honor you. It seems like You meant for her to be born. I don't understand." Then Jesus showed me a picture of Himself sitting on top of a tall building watching a parade on the street below. He said, "That parade is Time. I sit above it and know everything that will ever happen. I knew all the sins you would commit before you were born, as I do about everyone. And I have a redemption plan in place for every sin when people turn to me. You refused to have an abortion and Ginny's life is the Redemption Plan for that choice." Wow! He is still teaching in parables!

Another time He initiated the communion. A

couple of years ago I was walking from one room to another and suddenly I was overwhelmingly aware of the Father. He was so Holy and I was so unholy that I gasped, "WHY did you adopt me?" Then I felt that amazing love that I felt years ago from the Holy Spirit, and the Father said, "I adopted you BACK!" And I understood that we were all in His mind and heart before creation and He knew what we were like perfect, made in His image with the individual uniqueness He gave each of us as His children. When the fall came, He knew we would not be born perfect the way we were in His mind and heart, but He had the Plan to purchase us back to belong to Him and become the perfect individual He has loved before the beginning of Time. (I Peter 1:18,19)

That was probably the seed planted that led to the topic of this book.

# PART TWO

# LOVE

# Chapter Six
# Recognize and Reject Idols

Earlier we looked at what Jesus calls the main commandment, to love God with all our heart, mind, soul, and strength. In other words, we are to love Him with all we think, feel, want, and do. Anything we love more than Him in any way is an idol.

In John's first letter, he ends with the admonition: *"Little children, keep yourselves from idols."* (I John 5:21) John calls his reader "little children" several times but he is writing to all Christian people, because no matter our age, we are still children spiritually. He is writing to us, young and old, male and female. Keep yourselves from idols. What is an idol? We don't build statues to bow down to...well some people think that bowing down to a statue of Jesus is sinful. But mostly we think of statues of Buddha or Krishna or Ashtoreth or some other god other than the real God of the Bible.

The word idol is Greek – eidolon: a form for worship. That word can imply heathen gods, or it can imply anything that is more important to us than the Lord.

I remember a time I was asked to be part of a prayer team that was to stay in a room and pray during both days of a national Christian event. The event was held at Rupp Arena, the University of Kentucky's huge venue with basketball court and many conference and meeting rooms. Shortly after I arrived, a man from another state who was also to be a prayer warrior entered the room. The first thing he said was, "I was interested to come here because we all know that Kentuckians are idolaters who worship UK basketball." I was shocked but when I thought about it I realized what he was saying. I am not a sports fan of any kind and neither is my husband, but we certainly know many who are. The first thing that got me over my shock at his words was the memory of when the church I attended called off their Wednesday meeting because UK had a basketball game at the same time.

When my oldest daughter Ginny was in high school, she was invited to the prom. But I had no money for a prom dress. Every one we looked at was too expensive. And I remember considering how I could steal one. I was horrified when I realized what I was thinking. And I said to myself, "That is idolatry – putting a dress for Ginny above God's Word and Law." I repented. The very gracious Lord gave me enough money so that Ginny could pick out the material and pattern she wanted for a dress, and a wonderful seamstress made the dress at a reasonable price.

I also remember a time when my daughter Beth moved in with us along with her daughter who was only one year old. They were with us several years during and after the divorce. I got very close to that child as I kept her while her mother worked. It was a rough time in my life emotionally and that little girl was my greatest joy. Yes – not Jesus but Maggie. And one day when she was around three I realized that I had made an idol of her. I repented and began spending more time with Him. I realized later that I am not the only person who has had that problem, as evidenced by some of the phrases on cups or shirts about grandchildren being the best thing that ever happened. I love my grandchildren very much and I'm even closer to my daughters now, but they are not responsible for my joy in life.

Even more than them, I have grown to love the Lord: Father, Son, and Holy Spirit. But to get there involved making choices. As I mentioned earlier I was bombarded most of my life with an overwhelming desire for romance - not sex but romance. I wanted a man to love me the way Daddy loved my mother – which was probably idolatry. He would stroke her hair and look at my brother, sister, and me and say, "Isn't she the most beautiful thing you ever saw." I would smile and nod but what I was really thinking was, "No, the movie star Elizabeth Taylor is."

I have been married three times and divorced twice. I was not at fault about the divorces but getting into marriages that God did not intend was my fault. I've told you how the first one came about. We were married nine years and he was very abusive. But I took it because I had gotten pregnant and felt that I deserved the abuse. I got divorced when the abuse began to affect my two daughters. Then I married to a man who was wonderful to the girls and I thought how great for them to have a good father. I wasn't in love with him, but I married the "good Daddy." I found out later after we had a daughter of our own and had gotten custody of his two sons, that he was a child molester. Because of the sons having been given custody to the father by the judge "because of the stepmother" I stayed with him much longer than I should have. I finally left, again because of my children, after twelve years. The marriage I am in now has lasted thirty-eight years. That is because the Lord told me He ordained this marriage. I've learned that everything that calls itself marriage isn't. (By the way, I joked with my husband that based on mathematic progression of my first two marriages 9,12, I could promise to stay with him 15 years.)

The apostle Paul wrote to the church at Corinth concerning marriage and addressed three different sets of people 1. The unmarried and widowed 2. The married and 3. The rest! I was 'the rest' to whom he said if the unbelieving spouse wants to remain with them, let them stay. (I Corinthians 7:8-16) In other words, the believer and unbeliever were not married in God's eyes. I do not regret my two "wrong" marriages since I have three lovely daughters because of them. And I would like to say that my first husband, the former wife abuser, became a Christian after he had a massive stroke. He had to be fed and taken care of, but his mind worked perfectly. It was so sad. He came to the church I pastor several times with one of our daughters, and asked me to preach his mother's funeral. I visited him several times in the hospital before he died, and all was well. God is so good and when we choose the right way to do things, especially to forgive, He can work miracles.

We must keep ourselves from idols. With me one of the greatest idols ever in my life was pleasing other people. As I said earlier, refusing to have an abortion was probably the first time I ever refused to do anything someone wanted me to do. I was the ultimate people pleaser, and still have to fight that. It takes the Lord telling me, "No!" to stop me. One thing I learned is that sometimes we are not helping people but enabling them.

I am a people lover and rarely is there anyone I don't feel some fondness for. And I have always wanted to help the poor. I was a food stamp worker at one point in my life and the way I got into ministry was because I saw several examples of four generations of families living on welfare, which had become an idol to them. I resigned and began taking Christian puppet shows to housing projects to teach children that God loved them, and they could become anything they and He wanted them to be. I praise the Lord for that ministry. I don't know how many children were affected but I do know that years later one was a police officer and I ran into another who was attending seminary.

However, I have helped people who ended up expecting me to take care of them over and over; I brought in the homeless several times only to have them steal from me each time; and I learned that getting drug addicts out of jail just helped them get back on drugs more quickly.

There are so many things we make idols without realizing it. One of the ways we can identify them is to ask ourselves what we like to do best, more than spending time with the Lord. Play with our pets? Watch TV? Spend time on social media?

We don't think the desire to help people could be an idol, but when we realize it has a lot to do with our self-image, we need to repent, receive forgiveness, and determine to only do His will, at His instigation.

And that brings me to my favorite subject – forgiveness. When I am asked to speak to a church or group for the first time I preach on, "The Most Important Thing." And that is forgiveness. Receiving it, giving it, and forgiving yourself. The first time I spoke at a national conference, the subject was "Forgiveness."

# Chapter Seven
# Forgiveness: Give and Receive

We talked about receiving forgiveness from God in our first part of the Progression of Perfection, making Him our Lord. Now we are talking about making Him our Love. When we truly love Him, we want to be like Him, and He is the great Forgiver.

In my opinion, the scariest part of the Bible is when Jesus tells a story and explains it, recorded in Matthew 18:21-35. Peter came to Him and asked how many times he should forgive someone who sinned against him. Then he made

what he obviously thought was a generous answer, "Seven times?" Jesus must have really
shocked Peter with the answer "Seventy times
seven." Forgive the same person four hundred
and ninety times?

Then Jesus goes on to tell one of His teaching
parables (or it could have been a true story; we
are not told). He said the Kingdom of Heaven
works like this: A king brought in those servants
who owed him, to bring them to accountability.
One owed him the equivalent of over nine million
dollars. The man couldn't pay the debt, so the
king commanded him, his wife, his children, and
all he owned to be sold. The man fell on his face
and begged him, "Have patience and I will pay
you all I owe." So the king was "moved with compassion, and loosed him, and forgave him the
debt." Whew! That's a lot of compassion, forgiving over nine million dollars. He must have been
a rich king!

The man then left the presence of the king,
probably with great relief, and went and found a
fellow servant that owed him about fifteen dollars and took him by the throat and said, "Pay
me what you owe me!" But the servant fell down
at his feet and begged him, "Have patience and I
will pay you all I owe." Sound familiar? But the
forgiven one had his fellow servant cast into
prison.

When the king found out about this, he called

the one he had forgiven and said, "I forgave you all that debt because you wanted me to. Shouldn't you have had compassion on the one who owed you, the same way I pitied you?" And then comes the scariest two verses in God's Word, in my opinion.

"*And the king was angry and delivered the one he had forgiven over to the tormentors til he had paid all that was due him.* **So likewise shall my heavenly father do to you if you, from your hearts, do not forgive every one his brother their trespasses**." (Matthew 18:35, emphasis mine).

ARGHH! The first time I read that, I started forgiving, as quickly as I could, anyone who had ever done anything against me. If that doesn't motivate you to forgive, I can't think what would.

The only person I ever had a difficult time forgiving was the child molester. I was really struggling with that when the Lord showed me something.

I'd always wondered why it says Jesus was dead three days and three nights before His resurrection – Friday to Sunday is not three days. I still don't understand it completely but I'd noticed several years earlier that when He was in the garden of Gethsemane on Thursday night (Mark 14:33-36) Jesus began to be "*amazed and very heavy*" and He said to Peter, James, and John, "*My soul is exceeding sorrowful unto death...*" He then went on to pray that if possible the Father would take away what was going to happen. It's almost funny to hear the Son of God trying to persuade the Father by saying, "*Abba* (Daddy) *Father, all things are possible with you. Take this away from me. Nevertheless, not what I will but what you will.*" In other words, "You could save them some other way because You can do anything so don't make me do this. But (sigh) not what I want but what you want may come to pass." To me, that shows that Jesus' nature had already begun to change – He was no longer completely one with the Father. He had already begun to take on our sins; it didn't just start at the cross. He was amazed and heavy because He had never experienced the feelings of sin before. And He clearly said that His soul was sorrowful unto death. The death of Jesus started there, in the garden, in His soul – just as the first Adam's death began in a garden with the death of his soul, and his body didn't die for hundreds of years.

When I was trying to forgive the child molester, that came to my mind as well as Jesus asking God from the cross why He was forsaken. He wasn't forsaken of course; our sins separated Him from experiencing the Presence of the Father. Then the big revelation from Luke 23:34 when Jesus on the cross said, "Father, forgive them for they don't know what they do."

Some of you may think I made this up, but I believe with all my heart the Lord showed me then that if Jesus had not asked for the sins committed by and against us all to be forgiven, He would have been stuck with those sins for eternity and never risen from the dead. Then He told me that when we forgive, all the consequences of sin can be removed. I immediately saw Jesus on the cross bearing the punishment for all of us, even the child molester. And He took those sins off to hell and left them there (Acts 2:23-31) so when we agree with that forgiveness, we can be free from the results of those sins.

I forgave and contacted others who needed to forgive the man. The ones who were molested by that man had dramatic wonderful changes in life after they forgave, as did I.

Forgiveness – the most important thing. Receiving from God for ourselves and receiving from God for others.

I want us to look at what forgiveness really is – and isn't.

### Forgiveness Is Not a Feeling

1. Forgiveness **is not** excusing bad things that are done to you. Sin is sin, no matter what hurts or needs the person sinning may have. Don't excuse. It doesn't help you or them.

2. Forgiveness **is not** saying that the wrong thing didn't matter or that enough time has

passed away to make it okay. Just because something happened a long time ago doesn't mean that the effect of that harm isn't still with you – in your heart or mind or body or actions.

3. Forgiveness **is not** a restored relationship. Just because you have forgiven someone does not mean that your relationship with them is restored. You may forgive them, but you don't have to trust them and you don't have to like them; you just don't want them punished for what they did. There may come a time when they receive forgiveness and change and then God can restore the relationship, but it may never happen.

## Forgiveness Is a Choice

1. Forgiveness **is** deciding that punishment for the wrong is not demanded for the person who did it. Jesus bore the punishment for everyone.

2. Forgiveness **is** deciding that what was done can no longer affect you. Redemption is yours by Jesus Christ. He not only bore the punishment; He took the sin and it's results away. Let them go!

3. Forgiveness **is** putting the past in the past. And not talking about it anymore. Your words affect your emotions – don't bring back your pain.

One of the most difficult things to do is to

forgive yourself when you have caused harm to someone else and then realized the depths of your sin. I couldn't forgive myself about many things for years. Then I had a breakthrough.

I remember teaching about my breakthrough in a workshop at a different Aldersgate national conference than I mentioned before. I thought because I'm not famous that no one would show up. The topic was "Forgiveness, the Most Important Thing." I prayed that whoever needed to know more about forgiveness would be led to come. Hmm, I prayed correctly. The room was packed including those standing at the back. I taught what I've said here and then I came to the part about forgiving yourself. After the workshop a middle-aged man came up to me and said, "Thank you. When you said that to not forgive yourself is pride, I felt electricity go through my whole body. So after years, I finally did." Praise the Lord!

To not forgive yourself is to say in essence, "Others may be subject to that sin, but I should be above it." Pride. We are all subject to any sin. The Lord gave me a definition once that has helped me. "Humility is not a virtue. It is simply the realization of one's true state of being."

So recognize it. Laugh at your foolish pride, forgive yourself, and receive the forgiveness from God that was bought for you on the Cross by Jesus.

## Chapter Eight
## Worship Him

St. Bernard of Clairvaux said there are four progressions of love:

1. Man loves self for self's sake
2. Man loves God for self's sake
3. Man loves God for God's sake
4. Man loves self for God's sake.

Interesting. And I believe very true. We start out as babies, fallen self-centered beings who love ourselves and cry because of hunger, need for attention, pain, and anything else we want someone to take care of for us. Then as we grow and find out all God can do, we love Him so we will be in better condition, saved, healed, provided for, etc. Then we come to this part of the Progression we are in now – Man loves God, for God's sake. He has loved us so much, we want to make Him happy. Later, we realize that if He is going to do all He wants through us, we must love ourselves for His sake.

That fourth step is why we have to forgive ourselves and get on with it, which we will look at more deeply in the third part, Making Him Our Life. But right now I want us to look at number three. Man loves God for God's sake. There are two main ways we can do that, besides our actions of obedience and love to others. We commune with Him and we praise and worship Him in song.

I love worship. To me worship music is an intimate communication in song to the Lord while praise is singing about Him. I like praise too but when a worship song is sung, I usually end up on my knees.

For example: a praise hymn is, *His Name is Wonderful*. A worship hymn is, *Jesus, the Very Thought of Thee*.

A praise song is, *Great Is The Lord and Greatly to Be Praised*. A worship song is, *I Stand in Awe of You.*"

Some of my favorite praise songs are, *Majesty, O How He Loves You and Me, I Will Bless the Name of Jesus*. And some of my favorite worship songs are, *Lord, You're Beautiful, More Precious than Silver,* and *Father, I Adore You.*

Another favorite of mine is "Put a Fire down in my soul that I can't contain and I can't control. More of you, God, more of you." I'm not sure if that is praise or worship – to me it is simply a cry of the heart, a prayer of petition set to music.

Walter Savage Landor said, "Music is God's gift to man, the only art of Heaven given to earth, the only art of earth we take to Heaven." If I am discouraged, sad, rebellious, tempted, angry, I put a Christian music CD in my player and sing along. It literally changes my inner feelings. Bono said, "Music can change the world because it can change people." That is so true. And a love song sung to our Lord or about Him is pouring forth that love into the atmosphere.

We often don't realize how our feelings can change our surroundings. This had nothing to do with music, but I remember a time when I had a job that I liked okay except for our weekly meetings with the boss. They were so boring and irritating. One day I decided that I was going in and just think about how much God loves each one of the staff gathered, including the boss. I figured I'd ask for information about our instructions for the week from one of my co-workers later, but during the meeting I was only going to concentrate on God's love for everyone. And I did. Amazingly enough, about five minutes into the meeting, the boss cracked a joke, which shocked but relaxed everyone. Soon they were all sharing funny stories about things that happened with clients and enjoying each other. When the meeting was over I was walking out beside the woman who had sat next to me. I saw she had been doodling instead of taking notes. And what the paper had on it were dozens of hearts.

God's Love, even thought about, is the most powerful thing in the universe. Because God IS Love! When you are loving Him, you are bringing His Presence into your surroundings as well as your heart.

Did you ever wonder why God created man when He knew what was going to happen? We're told that Jesus was crucified from the foundation of the world. (Rev. 13:6). He knew when He created us that the Jesus/Yeshua/Salvation part of Himself would have to die to take away the sinful nature we received from the devil and make us true children of Abba/Father.

The reason is that God wanted a family. He is LOVE and love always wants to communicate with a beloved. He wants intimate time alone with each of His beloved children. You are His beloved and He wants intimate time alone with you.

Music combined with love lyrics is, to me, the easiest way to enter into that intimate time. He is longing for you more than you have ever longed for anyone. He is ONE – our Father, our Savior/Bridegroom, and our Counselor/ Lifechanger. He wants you to get to know Him better. He wants to become the Love of Your Life.

As I said earlier, my main problem in life has been romance. I longed for it from childhood. I wanted to be loved the way Daddy loved Mother. But I made a lot of mistakes and committed a lot of sins because of that longing. Until recently I couldn't imagine the Lord being the Love of My Life. There were two men who I honestly saw as that love of my life. Neither of them was a husband to me. When you are married, the harsh realities of personality come out and what was once huge romance can die away, even though love and commitment remain. But if you're never with the one you love, you don't see those day-to-day problems. The Lord finally got through to me that I had made an idol out of each of them at different times. That was awful and I repented. And that's when He showed me that He wanted to be the love of my life.

So instead of putting on romantic songs and playing them, I put on praise and worship music which stirs my heart into a passionate longing for Him.

There is a hymn written in 1876 by George Robinson, music by James Mountain, that is probably one of my favorites ever. I don't know whether it is praise or worship but even though it is not singing to Him except once, it causes me to worship. In fact, one of the first things I do in the morning is read the words before I get out of bed, and often at night also. I usually just read the first, third, and fourth verses. And I play it on my piano and sing along often in the daytime. I can print it here because the copyright status is public domain now.

1. Loved with everlasting love,
Led by grace that love to know;
Gracious Spirit from above,
Thou hast taught me it is so!
Oh, this full and perfect peace!
Oh, this transport all divine!
In a love which cannot cease,
I am His, and He is mine;

2. Heav'n above is softer blue,
Earth around is sweeter green;
Something lives in every hue
Christless eyes have never seen;
Birds with gladder songs o'erflow,
Flow'rs with deeper beauties shine,

Since I know, as now I know,
I am His, and He is mine;

3. Things that once were wild alarms
Cannot now disturb my rest,
Closed in everlasting arms,
Pillowed on His loving breast;
Oh, to lie forever here,
Doubt and care and self resign,
While He whispers in my ear
I am His, and He is mine;

4. His forever, only His;
Who the Lord and me shall part?
Ah, with what a rest of bliss
Christ can fill the loving heart!
Heav'n and earth may fade and flee,
Firstborn light in gloom decline,
But while God and I shall be,
I am His, and He is mine;

The song was based on Scripture, *"I am my beloved's and my beloved is mine..."* (Song of Solomon 6:3) and *"For I am persuaded that neither death, nor life, nor angels, nor principalities, nor powers, nor things present, nor things to come, nor height, nor depth, nor any other creature, shall be able to separate us from the love of God, which is in Christ Jesus, our Lord.* (Romans

8:38,39)

Try it. Say it out loud and let your heart connect with the words. And if you can play the piano or guitar, get the sheet music and sing it. I admit, it is the third verse that always really draws me closer into intimacy – "doubt and care and self resign." Whew! What a relief.

And of course, say the scriptures out loud also.

It makes Him happy when you feel His love and love Him back.

# Chapter Nine
# Love Others For Him

When I think of loving others for Him, I usually first think of forgiveness. We've already talked about that, and I hope you have forgiven everyone in your life who needed it.

But what else can we do to love others? That word love is *agape* – active good will. It doesn't mean be fond of or enjoy. So how can we have active good will toward others?

Loving those He has called to be the public vessels of His ministry in the earth, as in pastors, evangelists, teachers, worship leaders, etc., is obvious; you can help them by praying for them and blessing them financially. You can help them by telling others about what God is doing through them. You can attend their meetings and receive what God has to give you through them. You can buy their books or DVDs. I am not at all saying these are the most important ministries but they are some the Lord has me support and show His love to: Aldersgate Renewal Ministries (Methodist), Matt Chandler (Baptist), Bill Johnson (Pentecostal), and Rabbi KA Schneider (Messianic Jewish). I am very trans-denominational!

Loving friends is kind of obvious also but in different ways. Does someone need a ride to the doctor or the grocery? Do you have the means of doing that for them? A friend called me today to say that she wanted to furnish a meal for us and asked if I would want it tonight or tomorrow night. Do you ever feel that someone just needs a phone call to let them know you are thinking of them and care about them?

One of the best things you can do for anybody, family, friend, or acquaintance is to understand them. We are all different because we all have different backgrounds, different genetics, and different views of life. You may have people in your life that you don't understand and may not even like. Remember you don't have to like them to love them with God's kind of love.

But trying to understand them is one of the best things you can do.

The problems which debilitate people are because of wrong beliefs – lies about God, themselves, or others – which have been sown in their hearts by the father of lies. Hurting people are in pain because of things which have happened to them in the past and the beliefs about those things planted within their hearts. To know Truth with the mind does not stop the pain. The heart must have the lie rooted out.

I have prayed to be able to get miracles to people since I was six years old but one day just a decade or so ago, the Lord spoke to me while I was standing in my kitchen. "The greatest miracle you can get to people is to change their self-image." That wasn't the kind of miracle I had in mind but, considering my own life, I knew it was true.

Jesus said, *"Every plant which my heavenly Father has not planted shall be rooted up."* (Matthew 15:13). And we, the Body of Christ are part of that rooting up process. We are to show people how God sees them by letting Him love through us.

I never did anything right when I was a child. Born to two very athletic parents, I was the big disappointment. I remember when I was about four years old Mother told me I was going to start taking ballet lessons. Wow! I can't even describe my excitement and joy. I had visions of me in a pink tutu gracefully dancing on stage to an admiring audience. On my first day the teacher showed me to my locker and then went back to the desk to settle financial issues with Mother. I was so excited – ballet lessons and a locker. How grown up can you get? Then I heard my mother saying, "Her father and I don't expect you to teach her to dance but we hope you can help her be a little less clumsy." My dreams of being a dancer fell into a pit.

I loved people and I was always trying to reach out and be friendly. Two incidents come to mind, both when I was around three. One of my favorite things to do was to go downtown on the bus with my mother to the drugstore where I would get ice cream and she would shop for things like toothpaste and makeup. I noticed that when people got on the bus, they never spoke to the driver. They just gave him money and he gave them change which was in a little apron he wore with lots of pockets for the different denominations of coins. I finally thought of something to say to him. My mother had a dressing table skirt that had lots of pockets that she kept her hairbrush and other cosmetic items in. The next time we went on the bus, as mother handed him our bus fare, I smiled a great smile and said, "You look like my mother's dressing table." Silence from everybody and I was soon jerked away and back to our seats. I tried to explain but Mother just shook her head. I felt so foolish. Of course, he wouldn't understand about the apron resemblance to the dressing table. But I was too tongue tied to explain.

The other time was at the grocery store. We went weekly and I didn't know about the charge account which my parents paid off at the end of each month. I just noticed that everybody else in the line paid for their groceries, but we didn't. I wondered why and was embarrassed that Mother never thanked Mr. McGregor (I remembered his name because of Peter Rabbit). So one day I decided I'd thank him myself. We were about in the middle of a long line and I had time to decide how to word my gratitude. As Mother walked away with the groceries, I said, "Thank you, Mr. McGregor, for giving us our groceries every week." No, Mother didn't have a stroke or heart attack but the anger in her face made me decide never to say anything publicly again.

After that, no matter how I wanted to reach out to people, I didn't. I was told I couldn't say anything right and I believed it. Even with my close friends I kept my mouth shut. I knew anything I said would be stupid. If I disagreed with anybody, I assumed I was wrong.

One of my personal inner healing things happened with the Mr. McGregor incident. I tried to visualize what would have happened if Jesus had been there.

Tell my mother and the rest of the crowd that I didn't understand about charge accounts? No. That didn't work.

Be inside Mr. McGregor and smile at me and tell me about charge accounts? No that didn't work.

When I quit trying to make something up to heal the hurt inside, Jesus initiated a vision; it was very unexpected but it worked. I haven't felt the shame since and feel free inside.

I looked up at Mr. McGregor and said as before, "Thank you for giving us our groceries every week." He smiled back at me and said, "You're welcome."

Strange but when I thought about it, the Lord is truly the provider however He chooses to do it. Jesus was there in Mr. McGregor appreciating my gratitude.

The reason for all these stories is to show how a change of self-image can change a life. I saw myself as a failure, a klutz, someone who couldn't do or say anything right. But God changed me.

One of the 'outside my family' things that that added to my poor self-image was in first grade. The music teacher divided us into singing birds and listening birds. I was excited because I knew I would be a singing bird; my grandmother had always told me I'd grow up to be a blues singer.

I loved to sing! But no, the teacher designated me as a listening bird. The only thing listening birds got to do at the Christmas show where all our parents came was to snap our fingers at "Up on the housetop (click, click, click); down through the chimney comes Old Saint Nick." And there was no way this clumsy little girl could snap her fingers. Humiliation again.

That was the first incident redeemed by the Lord. At the beginning of my Junior year in high school, I was sitting on the steps with my friends during the lunch break and we were singing *Tell Me Why*. The music teacher walked by and turned around and called my name (which was Marilyn at the time) and said, "You need to be taking music lessons." Talk about humiliation! I needed to take music lessons just to sing with my friends? But it turned out that I was a contralto and she needed more alto and contralto singers in the chorus. She arranged with the principal that I could switch from my third year of taking art to my first year of taking music. That fall I was in a girls' quartet called "The Sweet Adelines" and then I made all-state- chorus. Wow. Later I realized why my first-grade teacher made me a Listening Bird – my voice was probably lower than even the boys at that age. And that made sense that my grandmother thought I would be a blues singer, with such a deep voice. I've sung in several church choirs over the years and while I'm certainly not the best, I'm happy about what God gifted me with – and redeemed.

Miss Eudora South, Frankfort High School's Music teacher, was one of those people used by the Lord to root out a very wrong self-image from me.

As for the speaking, that happened when I needed to get a job but had several children I didn't want to send to sitters after school. I became a Tupperware lady after having a party myself and loving the product and being persuaded by the one who sold. She convinced me that I could do it. And I thought that since I wouldn't be giving my own opinion but just telling facts about a great product, I could. And of course that was the beginning of public speaking that led to leading a youth group that led to teaching an adult Sunday School class, that led to writing and hosting Christian plays, to pastoring a church, to holding retreats and seminars, to speaking at national conventions. I remember once being asked to speak at a Jesus Rally in Louisville, KY many years ago. There were thousands of people and I wasn't the slightest bit nervous. That Tupperware lady, whose name I don't even remember, was the beginning of God rooting out my fear of speaking.

I can honestly say that if I say something I find out later was wrong, it doesn't bother me.

So what? I'm human; I make mistakes. Humility is simply the realization of one's true state of being. God is so good.

As far as the clumsiness, I hate to say it but that never changed much. However when my husband and best friend nicknamed me "Puddles," because I always stepped in puddles on the ground and on other things, I just laughed and said that my mind was on more important things than looking down at where I was walking. No more shame!

One of my dearest friends has been free from alcohol for decades but as we started doing some counseling about her childhood she discovered for the first time in her life why she had started turning to alcohol in the first place. She said that was one of the most freeing things that had happened to her. I was used to help root out some lies about herself.

Loving others. As Jesus told me, the greatest miracle you can get to someone is to change their self-image. Turn your day over to the Lord and watch for someone to help. Physically yes, but emotionally YES!

# Chapter Ten
# Loving Him Most!

*And thou shalt love the Lord thy God with all thy heart, and with all thy soul, and with all thy mind, and with all thy strength;' this is the first commandment.* (Mark 12:30)

I would speculate that most of us who are really dedicated Christians are somewhere in Part Two of our progression: Making Him Our Love. Once we really get to know Him, it is very easy to love Him. But loving Him the most? Acting good will toward Him more than our spouse, child, parents? How can we do that? How DO we do that?

Actually the answer is easy. Once we discover and realize that He loves our spouse, child, parent, more than we do, we can relax and love Him more than anyone or anything. He will take care of them and if He wants to use us to help them He will let us know. That is a very freeing revelation.

But as we've talked about before, what He wants most from us is intimacy. I read somewhere that there are seven components of intimacy between two beings.

1. Knowledge: we share our dreams, desires, goals etc. God has definitely though scripture shown us His, and He knows ours, but when we spend time alone with Him, He lets His dreams, desires, and goals be known to us on a deeper level until they become our own passions. Another of the ministers I respect is Leif Hetland who describes intimacy as "in-to-me-see." That is knowledge. And the Lord wants us to know Him as deeply as He knows us.

2. Interdependence: each one relies on the other. What? We of course rely on Him but Him rely on us? Yes, remember we are His Body in the earth today, just as Jesus was His Body in the earth two thousand years ago. Just as Jesus did the Father's will, He now relies on us to carry out His will.

3. Care: Genuine, selfless care of showing desire for the happiness and wellbeing of another is the third aspect listed of intimacy. God wants us to be happy and I believe, though His wellbeing is established, we grow in our desire for His happiness.

4. Trust: Confidence that the other will act honorably and beneficially toward us. That may sound simple but think about it. Have we grown in that understanding about our Lord? Or do we really think He might do something harmful to us – for our own good? I don't believe that. As we discussed earlier, Jesus said He came to give us abundant life. It is the enemy of God and mankind that comes to steal, kill, and destroy (John 10:10.) Now can God always trust us? Hmm. Well, we're getting there, right?

5. Responsiveness: Responding to the needs and desires of the other, causing them to feel appreciated and loved. God does that to us. And the more we get to know Him and His needs and desires, we can respond to what makes Him feel appreciated and loved.

6. Mutuality: A growing of close connection that changes the view from 'me' to 'we.' God already sees us that way – His children, His Beloved. And we'll discuss how we can grow in that understanding toward Him during our next part where we learn to Make Him Our Life.

7. Commitment: A desire and determination

for the relationship to grow and continue forever. Commitment helps the other six components of Intimacy to remain solid and become permanent.

One of my favorite worship songs I didn't mention earlier is "The Greatest Thing in All My Life" and goes on to say, "is knowing You," "loving You," "serving You." There is a progression of knowing Him, loving Him, and serving Him and those things are part of our progression of perfection. Getting to know Him better is fascinating. As I will tell about later I was surprised when I saw Jesus' prayer in the garden in a different light. There are other things in scripture that we read religiously but if we really stop and let the Holy Spirit open our eyes, we see things that we aren't really taught.

One that comes to mind is the time recorded in Luke 8:22-25 when Jesus told the disciples to take the ship over to the other side of the lake. Then He fell asleep in the back of the boat. A big storm happened, wind blowing and water getting in the boat and they "were in jeopardy." The disciples woke Jesus up and told Him they were dying. He got up and spoke to and stopped the wind and the wild water, and all was calm. Then He asked them, "*Where is your faith?*" Think about it. He was asleep, obviously tired and yet they woke Him up to calm the storm. Was He irritated when He asked, "Where is YOUR faith?"? I don't know if He was irritated but I think it's obvious He didn't want to be awakened; He wanted to know why they didn't calm the storm themselves.

There was another time when the disciples were having trouble on the water. Recorded in Mark 6:45-52, this took place right after Jesus had fed five thousand with five loaves of bread and two fishes. *"Immediately Jesus made his disciples get into the boat and go on ahead of him to Bethsaida, while he dismissed the crowd. After leaving them, he went up on a mountainside to pray. Later that night, the boat was in the middle of the lake, and he was alone on land. He saw the disciples straining at the oars, because the wind was against them. Shortly before dawn he went out to them, walking on the lake. He was about to pass by them, but when they saw him walking on the lake, they thought he was a ghost. They cried out, because they all saw him and were terrified. Immediately he spoke to them and said, 'Take courage! It is I. Don't be afraid.' Then he climbed into the boat with them, and the wind died down. They were completely amazed, for they had not understood about the loaves; their hearts were hardened."*

This reminded me of the forty years the Israelites wandered in the wilderness after God delivered them from Egypt. They worshipped Baal; they turned their back on Him over and over.

Can you imagine seeing Him part the Red Sea, lead them through, and then drown their enemies? And can you imagine not too long after that, making a golden calf to worship instead of worshipping Him. To read about those years between Egypt and entering the Promised Land is an amazing illustration of God's patience and mercy. And obviously that patience and mercy was still there in Jesus. The disciples' hearts were hardened. They didn't understand the power of God in Jesus when they watched Him take five loaves of bread and two fish and feed 5,000 men. He was going to walk by them on the water, as they were struggling in the wind, but He saw their fear of the wind and Himself and reacted with the compassion that is His nature. As soon as He got in the ship with them, the wind ceased. This time He didn't even have to say anything. Just His presence can calm the storms in our lives.

I learned an interesting thing about God many years ago when my daughter Susie was in high school. It was band parent's meeting night and I was running a little late. There was no one else around when I parked my car, so I was running toward the building from the parking lot. It was an icy night, not bad but just enough that I thought it was silly to run. I slowed down and a childlike desire to skip came over me. I began doing so and almost laughing at myself at my childishness. And then I became aware of my guardian angel, walking beside me on my right. There was no question in my mind who it was, and I knew he would stop me from falling if I slid. But the thing that really got me was his fascination with my behavior. I knew he was thinking that humans are like God with a sense of merriment and humor. That surprised me. I never thought about angel personality. I never thought about them being different from humans. But then I remembered two things. It is humanity that is made in the image of God. And I recalled the Lord's humor at me that time in the Presbyterian Church choir loft over my priority of sinfulness. God has a sense of humor and a playful merriment. No wonder the little children loved Jesus!

One of the biggest revelations I have ever experienced about the Lord's humor was during a time I was confused. I had written a letter to Hannah Hurnard, author of *Hind's Feet On High Places*, about the girl called Much Afraid who left the village of Much Trembling to go to the High Places with the Shepherd and receive a name change. That book meant a lot to me. My name was Marilyn, which stems from the Hebrew word *mara*, which means bitterness and rebellion. As I've said, my childhood had taught me that I was pretty much useless and while I didn't actively rebel, I was very bitter inside about my insecurity. I wrote the letter telling Ms. Hurnard how much her book meant to me and how my great desire was to write allegories and fiction like that to help people change and know the Lord. To my great surprise, she wrote back – from England. Instead of encouraging me to write, she said she could see me speaking and teaching people a lot. It upset me. I wanted to write. Yes, I was a Tupperware lady but teaching people publicly about Jesus was a whole different thing.

The next morning, I was out on the carport, which we used as a porch, having my devotional time. I complained to Jesus about public teaching and asked Him, "If I'm really supposed to do that, why don't I want to?" Then He appeared in front of me (I don't know if He was really there or it was a vision in my mind). He reached down and His hands went into my heart. When He pulled them out He was obviously holding something in both hands. I was curious and asked, "What is that?" He opened His hands and there was a little chicken there. Then He lifted His hands and the chicken flew away. I know chickens don't really fly but He did truly take the "chicken" from my heart. And I laughed at His humor in the way He did it.

Not too long after that as I was in my bedroom one night He spoke to me and said, "I am giving you a new name." I was excited since I didn't like the old Marilyn at all. "What is it?" I asked eagerly. No response. I asked again. Silence. Strange.

The next evening, I went to my ladies Bible Study/Prayer Group which met in homes. That time it was in my friend Mildred's home. Another friend, Sue, came up to me and glared at me. "I had a dream about you last night." She seemed angry so I was horrified at what I might have done in the dream. "What was the dream?" I asked. She said, "You were standing behind a pulpit and said, 'I am Amy.' I said 'No, you are Marilyn.' But no matter how often I said it, you just shook your head and smiled and said, 'I am Amy.'

Wow, I knew that was the name God gave me, so I told the group about what had happened the night before. Later we found out the name 'Amy' means Beloved. Praise the Lord. Not only did He take the little chicken from my heart, He changed me from 'Bitterness' to 'Beloved'. I believe He had Sue give me my new name so I wouldn't think I made it up.

How could you not love someone like Him? How could you not make Him the Love of Your Life?

# PART THREE

# LIFE

# Chapter Eleven
# You Are the Temple of the Holy Spirit

*What? Know ye not that your body is the temple of the Holy Ghost which is in you, which ye have of God, and ye are not your own? For ye are bought with a price: therefore glorify God in your body, and in your spirit, which are God's. (I Corinthians 6:19-20)*

I am a temple? What does that mean? I never researched the word before today but found out something interesting. And humbling. The word temple here and in John 2:19 where Jesus calls Himself a temple is the Greek word *naos*, which means "dwell, shrine, temple." But the other word temple, talking about the Temple in Jerusalem where the Holy Place was is *hieron* in Greek, and Strong's Concordance says the definition is "the entire precincts –where naos is the central sanctuary itself."

The part of the temple where people gathered and sacrificed and interacted with priests is called the Outer Court. Then there was the Holy Place, where the bread and candles and incense were and only priests could enter. Then, separated by a thick veil, there was the Holy of Holies where the Ark of the Covenant was, containing not only the manna, Aaron's rod, and the Ten Commandments (representing His provision, His leadership, and His Law) but the Presence of God Himself. Only the High Priest was allowed in there and only once a year. That was the "central sanctuary."

Wow! Jesus said He was the central sanctuary of the place of God, and then Paul writes that we are the central sanctuary.

That means God Himself dwells in us. I know we've been taught that, but have we stopped to think what it really means?

No wonder John tells us, *"He that saith he abideth in Him ought himself also so to walk, even as He walked."* (I John 2:6) God offered life to everyone but He didn't come in to live in everyone, not until Jesus purchased them and they ask Him in. I knew Jesus lives in me through the Holy Spirit, but I never thought about the entire Trinity. Our Abba, Father, living in us? We are now the Body of Christ and Jesus asked His disciples, *"Believest thou not that I am in the Father, and the Father in me? The words that I speak unto you I speak not of myself: but the Father that dwelleth in me, He doeth the works."* (John 14:10) And we are now like Him. That really makes me want to make Him my life.

How do we do that? I mean I know that He is the life inside me, meaning if He didn't give me the essence of life, I would die. But if He lives inside me, I am not only part of the Body of Christ (which means Anointed One) in the earth, I am the sanctuary of the Holy Spirit. And somehow the Father is there too because they are all one. They were all present when Jesus walked the earth – He said that He and the Father were one. But remember, He had to go off and pray too. Getting alone with the Father is more than just making Him our Lord or learning to love Him. Getting alone with our Father is what it means to pray in the name of Jesus.

The word name means nature. That's why God changed people's names as we see recorded in scripture: Abram to Abraham, Jacob to Israel, Saul to Paul. That's why He changed my name –

and I am still growing into my new name, learning to be His beloved. When we pray in the name of Jesus we are not just supposed to say those words "in Jesus' Name, Amen (which means *So be it!*)" as most of us do. We are to pray in the nature of the Savior. We are to realize that we are the Beloved Child of our Abba, Father, an intimate offspring of the Creator. We ask as His beloved child, like Jesus did. And when we do that, we can expect to receive – if we ask what He wants and has promised us.

Jesus didn't ask anything that wasn't the Father's will, except once in the Garden of Gethsemane, and then He said, "not my will but Yours be done." Well, it just hit me, we don't know what happened in Jesus life between the ages of twelve and thirty. There may be many times in those eighteen years He prayed, "not my will but Yours be done" since He was tempted as we are in every way. (Hebrews 4:15) (I could feel His humor as I wrote that last sentence!) And I recently read where sometimes we Christians say sincerely, "not my will but Thine be done." And sometimes it's more like, "Okay, have it Your way!"

We are to realize that we are the containers of God in the earth. That's beyond my mental comprehension but my heart is beginning to realize it. And I'm seeing that as we grow in that knowledge, we are increasingly able to make

Him our Life.

We are to become, as Jesus was, a living Word of God. That is part of the process of perfection as we faithfully read, reflect, respond, and rest in God's written Word. And when we choose that resting in God's Presence is a regular part of our daily lives, we become a channel of God's presence to others.

Living in union with God, we are able to transcend ourselves as the center of life and experience all in God and God in all. Our energy becomes one with the Divine Energy. We become merciful, compassionate, and loving as He is merciful, compassionate, and loving.

*But we all, with open face beholding as in a glass the glory of the Lord, are changed into the same image from glory to glory, by the Spirit of the Lord.* (II Corinthians 3:18) The word glory, according to the Abrahamic religions, is used to describe the manifestation of God's Presence as perceived by humans. That means that as you keep your eyes on Him and believe He is changing you progressively into His image, other humans will experience His Presence through you.

# Chapter Twelve
# Fruits Of The Spirit

In this chapter I want us to discuss the fruits of the Spirit. And most of all I want us to see what that really means. We are called "*trees of righteousness, the planting of the Lord, that He may be glorified.*" (Isaiah 61:3) The Father planted us, a new seed of life by Christ Jesus. And then the Holy Spirit brings forth the fruit which is the nature of that seed.

The Holy Spirit lives in you and the fruits are what grow out into your soul as you turn your life over to Him. I saw a saying the other day,

"Gifts are freely given. Fruits are the result of a process. With spiritual gifts the Holy Spirit gives; while with spiritual fruit He gets." Think about it.

The fruits of the Spirit are the nature of God taking over our souls as we offer Him our wills, minds, and emotions, until we are fully His. It is definitely a process but one day we will be exactly like Him. We just read that He said so. *"But we all, with open face beholding as in a glass the glory of the Lord, are changed into the same image from glory to glory, even as by the Spirit of the Lord."* (II Corinthians 3:18)

Glory is an interesting word. In the Greek it is *doxa* meaning glory, honor, praise, worship, glorious. How can that apply to us? I believe that as we look at our Lord seeing His honor, how honorable He is, seeing what He deserves in praise and worship, seeing how gloriously wonderful He is, and if we keep our eyes on Him, recognizing that we are to be like Him, as though we are looking in a mirror, the Holy Spirit changes us from one degree of His nature to another. And one day we will be like Him.

The fruits of the Spirit are how our nature changes to be completely one with God.

*"But the fruit of the Spirit is love, joy, peace, longsuffering, gentleness, goodness, faith, meekness, temperance: against such there is no law. And they that are Christ's have crucified the flesh*

*with the affections and lusts. If we live in the Spirit, let us also walk in the Spirit."* (Galatians 5:22-25)

As we see, we must crucify our flesh to allow the fruits of the Spirit to grow in us. Crucify, *stauroo*, means to impale on a cross, to extinguish. Paul said earlier in his letter to the Galatians that he is crucified with Christ, *"nevertheless I live; yet not I but Christ liveth in me: and the life which I now live in the flesh I live by the faith of the Son of God, who loved me, and gave Himself for me."* (Gal 2:20)

That is a great relief if you think about it. Jesus Christ has faith that you will be able to extinguish your fleshly passions and let His own nature grow and take over your will, mind, and emotions! Yay! Thank you, Jesus!

Now let's look at those fruits and how they apply to our life.

The first fruit listed is love. Some people think that the passage means the fruit of the Spirit is love and all the other attributes mentioned are parts of love. That is true because God is Love so of course the fruit growing in us from Himself is Love. But I think it also can stand by itself as a fruit. Love is in the Greek *agape* and means several things. One of the definitions in the plural means a love-feast. I love that – we together, the Body of Christ, when submitted fully to Him and changed into His image, are a love feast! Other singular definitions are benevolence – meaning a desire to do good – affection, and charity.

As we look at Jesus we see that. Since He is the part of God who became human, we can look at Him to see how we are to act. He is definitely benevolent, so quick to heal and feed and help anyone who came to Him, it's obviously what He desired. And He was affectionate, having three best friends – Peter, James, and John, and evidently feeling affection for the children who came to Him, as well as others. And if charity means giving, He gave everything including His life.

So that is our goal, to walk like Jesus, loving as He did, as He does.

What comes against love becoming a part of ourselves? There are people we see that don't deserve good things done to them, so we have no desire to be benevolent. Affection means a feeling of fondness or liking. Have you ever met anyone who is impossible to like? And charity? Are we willing to give someone our car if they don't have one? As we talked about earlier, we don't want to enable people who have a dependency problem, but what if the Holy Spirit asks you to act out those things, benevolence, affection, charity, even when you don't feel them. Be willing but also be certain it is the Holy Spirit leading you and not some sense of religious obligation, or guilt. I think I chose the car question because that has literally happened to me – on both sides. I was once given a car, and I once gave my car to someone. Both times were acts of love!

The second fruit mentioned is joy. In the Greek that is *chara* meaning cheerfulness, calm delight, gladness. In Nehemiah 8:10, it says, "the joy of the Lord is your strength" and the word in Hebrew means gladness also. That helps, doesn't it? When you are in a difficult situation and on your own and you can't feel cheerful or glad, remember that He lives inside you and He is always glad. Why? Because He knows the end of the story. His calm delight in your future is your strength.

Years ago, a definition of joy came to my mind, "Joy is sorrow overcome; Joy is Love triumphant!" That definition helped in troublesome times. And once when I was out early in the morning alone at St. Augustine Beach in Florida, I was feeling a calm delight in the beach and the ocean and His Presence. Then He said to me, "This is what joy was like before the fall of mankind." Wow, nothing sorrowful to overcome, nothing bad to be triumphant over. Just calm delight in being with our Creator and His creation. Let His joy grow in your heart and pour out to those around you.

The third fruit mentioned is peace. That word

does not just mean lack of strife or an end to war. In Greek peace is *irene*, from a primary verb, to join, and this peace means one, quietness, rest, set at one again. So the peace which is the fruit of the Holy Spirit is that we can quietly rest in our Abba's love knowing we are one with Him and all is or will be well. I believe peace is the thing we all desire most – to be able to live in an attitude of rest knowing "the battle is not yours but God's." (II Chronicles 20:15) And He has already won your battles in the spirit realm.

That definitely leads to the fourth fruit longsuffering. The word in Greek is *makrothymia* and I'm glad I just have to write it instead of pronounce it! It means both patience and fortitude. Patience is capacity to accept or tolerate delay, trouble or suffering without getting angry or upset. Uh oh! I believe I have failed to produce this fruit many times. How about you? Fortitude means courage in pain or adversity. Well, I've done better on this part of the fruit but definitely with the help of the Holy Spirit.

The fifth fruit listed is gentleness. In the Greek it is *chrestotes* meaning gentleness and kindness. This is a fruit of God's nature which has to do with how we treat other people. Even when you need to correct them you are to do it gently and kindly. The first thing that came to my mind are parents. Often parents wound their children and give them a wrong image of God by disciplining harshly and unkindly. We usually get our idea of what God is like by what our parents are like. So parents, please definitely discipline, but do it with kindness and gentleness. And we are all to be gentle and kind to everyone.

Goodness is the sixth fruit. Again, I am glad I'm not speaking; the word in Greek is *agathosyne*. The definition is virtue and benevolence, goodness. Virtue means to have high moral standards and for a Christian, that means doing God's will and not our own. Benevolence is being well meaning. Goodness is to want to do God's will and have our rules of living be based on His moral standards.

The seventh fruit is faith. Faith is *pistis* in the Greek and one of the definitions is an assurance of the truthfulness of God. I love that – Scripture is given so you would know His nature and His promises, and then know how to pray and how to rely on Him, which is the second definition – reliance on Christ. It also includes our fidelity or faithfulness to Him.

Meekness is the eighth fruit listed, *praotis* in Greek. It means humility. We talked about that in the part about forgiveness, but I want to repeat what I wrote there. "Humility is not a virtue. It is simply the realization of one's true state of being." I have made so many mistakes and been forgiven for so many sins that I can honestly say that this particular fruit is easy for me to receive.

I know without a doubt that any goodness, ability, accomplishment through me is Him. And if you recall, Jesus walked in this fruit. He gave credit for everything He did to the Father.

The ninth and last fruit mentioned is temperance. In the Greek it is *enkrateia*, and no, I can't pronounce that either. Many people think that means self-control and other say it must mean Spirit control, but the word that it derives from means to exercise self-restraint. So I really believe that what it means is that we have the ability to restrain ourselves from wrong actions as we allow the nature of the Holy Spirit to give us that strength and pour that ability into our souls.

Okay, there you go. There is your new nature, your real nature, made in the image of God. And all you have to do is let the Holy Spirit work that nature, already in you because of your rebirth, out into your soul: your mind, will, and emotions.

# Chapter
# Thirteen Chosen

*Blessed be the God and Father of our Lord Jesus Christ who hath blessed us with all spiritual blessings in heavenly places in Christ: according as He hath chosen us in Him before the foundation of the world, that we should be holy and without blame before Him in love. Having predestinated us unto the adoption of children by Jesus Christ to Himself, according to the good pleasure of His will to the praise of the glory of His grace, wherein He hath made us accepted in the beloved. In whom we have redemption through His blood, the forgiveness of sins, according to the riches of His grace.* (Ephesians 1: 3-7)

Some people see this which talks about predestination and adoption and being chosen as proof that mankind has no choice in whether they will be in heaven forever or not. They believe God chose beforehand who will be saved and who won't. They also use Romans 8:29 to prove their point, *"For whom He did foreknow, He also did predestinate to be conformed to the image of His Son, that He might be the firstborn among many brethren. Moreover whom He did predestinate, them He also called; and whom He called, them He also justified: and whom He justified, them He also glorified."*

According to these scriptures, from that point of view, before the world began, God had already planned that you would be adopted back from sin and made a child in Jesus Christ through His death and forgiveness. God also planned that you would become like Jesus and called to do certain things and made you filled with an honor and praiseworthy nature. You didn't have anything to do with it. He planned it!

But what about what Jesus said? *"...even so must the Son of man be lifted up, that whosoever believeth in Him should not perish, but have everlasting life. For God so loved the world that He gave His only begotten Son that whosoever believeth in Him should not perish but have ever-lasting life. For God sent not His Son into the world to condemn the world; but that the world through Him might be saved. He that believeth on Him is not condemned but he that believeth not is condemned already, because he hath not believed in the name of the only begotten Son of God. And this is the condemnation, that light is come into the world, and men loved darkness rather than light, because their deeds were evil."* (John 3:14-19) And John wrote in I John 4:14,15: *"And we have seen and do testify that the Father sent the Son to be the Savior of the world. Whosoever shall confess that Jesus is the Son of God, God dwelleth in him, and he in God."*

According to these scriptures, Jesus was sent from the Father to save the whole world, not just some that God chose before the world began. Whether they become saved from sin and be new creatures in Christ is said to be their choice. God gave man free will. Believe in your need for a Savior, believe God provided Jesus for that purpose, and confess that Jesus is God's Son who died for you – and you are in, Bro! Right?

How in the world can we reconcile those two views to make sense?

If I had not had that vision of Jesus on top of the roof seeing the Parade of Time go by and knowing every sin each of us would commit, I wouldn't even begin to understand it. But that came to my mind and I thought, "What if God looked ahead in time at all the humans who would be born and saw which would believe in their need for a Savior and would believe in Jesus being that Savior. Then He would choose those believers for a role in the Body of Christ and adopt them back from the fallen lifestyle to be the children He envisioned from the beginning." I thought I had a great revelation, melding the two views.

Then I researched 'doctrine of election' on Wikepedia and found that others had figured this out long before I did. "Unconditional election (also known as unconditional grace) is a Reformed doctrine relating to predestination that describes the actions and motives of God in eternity past, before he created the world, where he predestined some people to receive salvation, the elect, and the rest he left to continue in their sins and receive the just punishment, eternal damnation, for their transgressions of God's law as outlined in the old and new Testaments of the Bible. God made these choices according to his own purposes apart from any conditions or qualities related to those persons.

The counter-view to unconditional election is Conditional election, the belief that **God chooses for eternal salvation those who he foreknows will exercise their free will to respond to God's prevenient grace with faith in**

**Christst**."

But even if that settles the confusion about the views of election and free will, some questions remain. Jesus said, *"Verily, verily, I say unto thee Except a man be born of water and of the Spirit, he cannot enter into the kingdom of God. That which is born of flesh is flesh and that which is born of the Spirit is spirit. Marvel not that I said unto thee, Ye must be born again."* (John 3:5-7).

Some people think that to be born of water and the Spirit means baptism in water and the Spirit. Personally, my opinion is that He is talking about the water of the Word. (John 15:3; Ephesians 5:26) *"Now you are clean through the word which I have spoken unto you." "That He might sanctify and cleanse it by the washing of water by the word."* But that's just my opinion of a side issue.

The main question to me is, 'If we are born again, why do we have to be adopted?'

The only conclusion I could come to is this: What if it's the opposite way around? What if He adopts us back (Prevenient grace – or grace before we accept Him) and then when we agree to that adoption, agree to belonging to Him by the sacrifice of Jesus for our sins (Justifying grace), the life giving Spirit pours the nature of Jesus Christ into our spirits and rebirth is accomplished.

Then our progress of perfection begins (sanctifying grace). I have just listed John Wesley's stages of grace, Prevenient, Justifying, and Sanctifying, which I fully believe in. Wesley was the original founder of the Methodist Church, and the Book of Discipline of that denomination defines grace as "the undeserved, unmerited, and loving action of God in human existence through the ever-present Holy Spirit." That grace was there before we knew about Him, it was there as we became saved, it is there as we are in our progression of perfection. Complete holiness, 'a life of godliness and holy devotion to God', is our goal. And we can't do it alone; we are completely dependent on the undeserved, unmerited, and loving action of God through the ever-present Holy Spirit.

## Chapter Fourteen
## How the World Works

Okay, remember at the beginning I said we were through with science for now – well, we are back, that 'now' is over. And please don't skip this part because in order to make Him your Life, you really need to know how this world works, as God made it to work.

We looked at how Daniel, Shadrach, Meshack, and Abednigo understood science as well as their other attributes. That was a help in exercising their faith to overcome the horrible worldly circumstances they were thrown into.

(Thrown into literally – into the lion's den and into the fiery furnace, and, by the way, the men who threw them into it died because of the flame). When the three followers of God came out they didn't even smell like smoke, and Daniel was not only not eaten but didn't have a scratch from the lions. We don't know what happened in the lion's den but we do know that there was a fourth man walking with them in the midst of the furnace who looked to the King "like the Son of God." (Daniel 3:22-25)

Do you know how this world works? I want to write again what I said in Chapter One.

Genesis 1: 1 *In the beginning God created the heaven and the earth. 2. And the earth was without form and void; and darkness was upon the face of the deep. And the Spirit of God moved upon the face of the waters. 3. And God said, "Let there be light": and there was light.*

1.The Father created atoms 2. The Holy Spirit hovered over them (made waves) 3. And the Son (the Word of God) spoke as to how those atoms were to come together – "Light BE."

When I demonstrate this at the talks I've given on "Quantum Physics and the Bible," I put out a lemon cake mix, an egg (hardboiled so it won't make a mess if dropped), a bottle of water, some oil, macaroni and cheese mix, a box of raisins, a box of grits, a jar of olives, a can of beef broth, and a can of tuna. Then I put my hand out and wave it over the table. I ask the crowd, ingredient by ingredient, would this go into making a cake. When they have chosen the first four ingredients. I say, "Cake be!" and pick them up. And then I say, "And Cake Be's!" Of course, I didn't have a miraculous baked cake but that is a simple demonstration of how God created in the first place and still does.

For matter to exist there must be, according to science, 1. Nuclear Forces 2. Gravitational Forces 3. Electromagnetic Forces. Now before your eyes cross as mine did when I first read that, let's look at those things in light of God's Word.

Nuclear forces would be atomic particles – like those that the Father created in the beginning. Gravitational forces are vibrations, like the Holy Spirit hovering (which means vibrated). Electromagnetic forces (sound waves) are when the Son spoke "Light Be!" And Light was.

Light energy is made up of waves and particles. Waves are the possibilities that may become matter. Particles are when those possibilities become solid in the physical realm.

God is the same yesterday, today, and forever. He still works the same way. He has created innumerable possibilities in this created world. His Holy Spirit is waiting to see which the Word will speak so His power can bring them to pass. (I suggest reading this paragraph again.)

Words spoken out by humans made in the image of God change light waves into particles – possibilities into reality. This is true about all humans, but unfortunately most of those realities are not God's will. Although Jesus and many others in the written Word tried to tell us how important our words are, we somehow "don't get it!"

I'm going to list just a few scriptures about the words of our mouth.

*He who guards his mouth and his tongue keeps himself from calamity.* (Proverbs 21:23)

*Life and death are in the power of the tongue...* (Proverbs 18:21)

*The tongue is a fire...a world of evil among the parts of the body...and is itself set on fire by hell.* (James 3:6)

Your enemy, the devil, comes at your mind with fear and anger in order to get you to speak out his will instead of God's will. He knows you are made in God's image. He tried to be above God by speaking out words to exalt himself but that was when he fell from his place of honor with God. (See Isaiah 14: 12-17) He is not able to speak out his will and get it to come to pass, but he gets you to speak it out when possible. He hates it when you speak out God's will.

Now let's look at three things Jesus said about words. The first one is amazing. Jesus lived in a world where Jewish law included forbidden food, including pork and shrimp – and I am so glad that law was done away with. But even then, Jesus said…

*What goes into a man's mouth does not make him unclean, but what comes out of his mouth, that is what makes him unclean.* (Matthew 15:11) Can you imagine the Pharisee's reaction to that one?

*It is the Spirit that gives life…the words I speak to you are spirit and they are life.* (John 6:63)

*Sanctify them by the truth. Your Word is truth. As you sent me into the world, I have sent them into the world.* (John 17:17,18)

And then Mark writes (Mark 16:20) *Then the disciples went out and preached everywhere, and the Lord worked with them and confirmed His word by the signs which accompanied it.*

That last is what you are called to do in this life. We are all called to be His disciples - those that follow Him and study Him. And we are all called to preach – proclaim the good news about the eternal Salvation He offers as well as the Healing, Provision, Wisdom, and other promises God gives to those who have faith in Him.

The other thing I've studied, not much but a little, are Parallel Universes. Personally, I believe there are only two – well, three if you count hell. I believe that heaven is the Spirit Realm, not someplace in this created universe. And of course there is the created universe that we live in physically, partially know, and study.

Ephesians 2:5-7 tells us that we were made alive in Christ and seated with Him in heavenly places. The Lord spoke to me once and said, "When you understand how the place I live works and how the place you live works and how you and I can both be in both places at the same time, you will see miracles happen and they won't seem like miracles at all." Unfortunately, I'm not there yet. I 'know' it partially – both places work by the Word of God - but I don't yet 'understand' it. However, since He used the word 'when' and not 'if', I believe I will get there. And you will too!

The first part of the Body of Christ, the early church, understood it. Phillip was translated to another place without going there physically (Acts 8:39). Paul spoke and the sorcerer Elymas became blind (Acts 13:1-12). Paul also healed many by speaking the Word of God and caused an earthquake and a prison to open when he and Silas prayed and sang.

And when you think about it, even though the new birth had not happened and Shadrach, Meshach, and Abednigo weren't spiritually 'in heavenly places', Jesus was there in the furnace with them as well as in Heaven.

And He is here, now. He said, *"Behold, I am with you always, even unto the end of the age."*

(Matthew 28:20)

He is here with you and you are seated with Him in heavenly places.

You are His physical body on the earth. Jesus said, *"You are the light of the world...Let your light so shine before men, that they may see your good works, and glorify your Father which is in heaven."* (Matthew 5:14,16)

For you to make Him your life, you need to understand that God has not changed. He created the universe with His Word, and He turned that world over to mankind's authority. When the enemy deceived mankind, he then began to get use of mankind's authority by getting them to speak out things that were not God's will. God purchased us who have physical bodies back from that fallen state in order to speak through us and bring His will about. You are a part of that physical body, the Body of Christ, the physical vessel of the anointing.

When you speak God's Word and His Will with the faith of Jesus that the spoken Word will happen, His Holy Spirit is able to bring that Word to pass in the world.

# Chapter Fifteen
## Stay In The Spirit

We have talked about making Jesus Christ our Lord by receiving the salvation He bought for us and learning His will through reading the written Word of God and listening to those who teach about it. We've talked about making Him our Love by rejecting idols, learning to forgive, and worshipping Him. Now we are talking about making Him our Life.

In this section we've looked at how we are supposed to live, letting the fruits of the Spirit take over the fallen nature in our wills, minds, and emotions, learning to realize that we truly belong to God and are the Body of the anointing in the earth, the temple of the Holy Spirit, as was Jesus. We are to walk as He walked (I John 2:6) and talk as He talked! We've learned that God hasn't changed the way He does things and because you now are the physical vessel of His voice in the world, that is a huge way you make Him your life.

I don't believe any of us are perfect yet. But many of us want to be because we are in love with God; we want to make Him happy.

How can we stay in the Spirit at all times, being attuned to His leading through every moment of our busy lives? I believe much of it has to do with what we do in our spare time. Do we read our Bibles and other Christian material, immerse ourselves into praise and worship music, take time to be still and grow in intimacy with Him?

I mentioned my encounter with the Father where He told me He adopted me back from my fallen nature. That was the first time I was completely overwhelmed by the Father's Presence and Love. And I have to admit that as I wrote this book, my love for Him as Father has grown.

It's to the point that I do call Him Abba when I talk to Him or write to Him, instead of always writing to the Jesus part of Himself, in my daily prayer journal. A lot of people I know call Him

"Papa" but for some reason, that doesn't resonate with me. I think it is wonderful, but I love the verse Romans 8:15, *"ye have received the Spirit of adoption, whereby we cry Abba, Father."* Abba is used to talk to instead of talk about. You can talk about Father, but when you talk to Him, you say Abba. *"And because you are sons, God hath sent forth the Spirit of God into your hearts, crying Abba, Father!"* (Galatians 4:6)

Did you catch the wording "crying" Abba, Father? The same word is used in both Romans and Galatians. The word cry and crying is *krazo* in the Greek and means to "call aloud (shriek, exclaim, intreat) – cry (out)." And Strong's says, "sometimes it's a scream." Interesting. When we saw Jesus using that term, He was intreating the Father to take away His calling to sacrifice His life for us. So it's okay for us to cry out to Him the same way. We can also cry out to Him exclaiming our love for him, our gratitude, or simply asking for His help.

But whether we are talking to the Father or the Son, it's important to stay in touch. And of course, that is done easily when we so choose, because His Holy Spirit lives inside us. What an honor!

Again, I grow in my realization of the Holy Spirit as a Person, the third Person of God. That really sounds strange to people but if you think about it, I am three people, a wife, a mother, and a minister. I am one person, but all of those roles have different meanings and actions. I know you who are reading this have differing roles in life. We actually usually have more than three! I could have gone on with grandmother, friend, neighbor, writer, painter etc.

God is one but He has three Persons in that oneness. When we connect with one of those Persons, we really are connecting with all three, which is not true about us humans.

Actually, the Trinity, or God in three persons is not just like we are with differing roles; it's much deeper than that. There really are three separate persons, as evidenced by Jesus praying to the Father on many occasions, even though He says, *"I and the Father are one."* (John 10:30) And the Holy Spirit is a person also. It is a great mystery that we humans cannot understand yet, even though we know it is true.

Staying in the Spirit at all times really means staying connected with God at all times, Father, Son, and Holy Spirit. Being connected with Him at all times means letting Him live out His will and life through us at all times. Think about it: you are a Child of the Father, part of the Body of Christ, and the Temple of the Holy Spirit. You are special!

I want to look at eight verses from Ephesians Chapter Three, beginning with verse 14. Paul is praying for the church.

*For this cause I bow my knees unto the Father of our Lord Jesus Christ, of whom the whole family in heaven and earth is named.* (14,15)

*That He would grant you, according to the riches of His glory, to be strengthened with might by His Spirit in the inner man.* (16)

*That Christ may dwell in your hearts by faith; that ye, being rooted and grounded in love,* (17)

*May be able to comprehend with all saints what is the breadth, and length, and depth, and height. And to know the love of Christ, which passeth knowledge, that ye might be filled with all the fullness of God.* (18,19)

*Now unto Him that is able to do exceeding abundantly above all that we ask or think, according to the power that worketh in us, unto Him be glory in the church by Christ Jesus throughout all ages, world without end. Amen.* (20,21)

I started to suggest you read the whole chapter and then I thought, no, I suggest you read the whole letter to the Church at Ephesus – many times. It is my favorite of the letters. It is the one that teaches us we are seated in heavenly places in Christ Jesus and the one that gives us the armor of God, which we will look at briefly later. Right now, I want to look closely at these verses.

*For this cause I bow my knees unto the Father of our Lord Jesus Christ, of whom the whole family in heaven and earth is named.* (14,15) You are part of the family of God and are named after Him. Remember that the word name means nature, or literally in this passage "to assign a character." You were assigned the character of the Lord Jesus Christ when you gave your life to Him.

*That He would grant you, according to the riches of His glory, to be strengthened with might by His Spirit in the inner man.* (16) Paul prays that you would be strengthened mightily inside, not according to your belief or goodness but according to the riches of His glory. He wants you to be strong like Jesus, choosing the Father's will at all times. And He gives you the ability, according to the abundance of His honor, to receive that strength by His Spirit.

*That Christ may dwell in your hearts by faith; that ye, being rooted and grounded in love,* (17) Wow, that strength that the Spirit gives you from the Father, allows the Anointed One to dwell in your hearts by faith. Believe He is there! Always. There are six different Greek words translated 'dwell' but this one is *katoikea* (yeah, you pronounce it) and it means 'to dwell permanently'. And when this permanent dwelling of the Lord Jesus Christ in our hearts is accomplished, we are rooted and grounded in love. Rooted and grounded – reminds me of the parable of the sower sowing the Word. The Living Word is now sown in the good ground of your heart and you will see great results.

*May be able to comprehend with all saints what is the breadth, and length, and depth, and height. And to know the love of Christ, which passeth knowledge, that ye might be filled with all the fullness of God.* (18,19) When you are rooted and grounded in love you will be able to (are you ready? Comprehend – Greek: *katalambano*) eagerly take and perceive 'with all saints' the love of Christ. Did you get that? You and I are part of a body of believers and it takes our interaction and cooperation with each other to truly get to that intimacy with the Lord that we desire. But when we do, when we work in love with the rest of our family, we will eventually be filled with all the fullness of God. THAT is your calling, that is making Him your life.

*Now unto Him that is able to do exceeding abundantly above all that we ask or think, according to the power that worketh in us, unto Him be glory in the church by Christ Jesus throughout all ages, world without end. Amen.* (20,21) Can you imagine that God is able to do way more than you can ask Him to do, or even think to ask, "according to the power that works in you"? Submit to the Lordship, the Love, the Presence of Him and let that power be complete. He will bless you beyond your own desires. Paul ends this prayer with his desire that by Christ Jesus, God's glory will be in the church throughout all ages. That is you, that is us.

I said we would look at the armor of God briefly which is listed in Ephesians 6:10-18. I haven't mentioned our enemy the devil much because I don't want to give him a lot of attention – he loves attention. But we are to know how to keep ourselves safe from the enemy.

Paul writes *Finally, my brethren, be strong in the Lord, and in the power of His might. Put on the whole armour of God, that ye may be able to stand against the wiles of the devil. For we wrestle not against flesh and blood, but against principalities, against powers, against the rulers of the darkness of this world, against spiritual wickedness in high places.* Did you notice that he starts out with the instruction to be strong in the Lord and in the power of His might? That is exactly what He told us about how to receive in his prayer in chapter three. This is the same letter, so he knows that you have been taught how to be strong in the Lord and His power – by trusting Him and letting Him reign in your heart. Then he says that we must stand against the "wiles" of the devil. The word wiles in the Greek is *methodeia* and means trickery and to lie in wait. The enemy is always trying to trick us. He hates us because we are the Body of Christ, the Temple of the Holy Spirit, the children of the Father.

Paul goes on to say that we are not wrestling

with flesh and blood. Think about that – the person that hurts you, steals from you, gossips about you, they are not what you are fighting. It is the spiritual wickedness that motivates and uses them. A principality is a chief, powers are strength. We humans give evil the power to be in control over the dictates of ourselves and our nations. We've given evil a lot of power in the last century – Abortion, Sexual Immorality, Cessation of Public Prayer, etc. And they now rule over this world; darkness has cast itself over the Light of the World in many areas. And the spiritual wickedness in the spirit realm constantly tries to affect the minds and hearts of everyone.

Paul lists the armor of God. I believe this means God is our armor. He is our Truth, our Righteousness, our Peace, our Salvation, our Sword. And we are to look to Him always for help in every situation.

We are to have our loins girt with the truth. Loins, *osphys* in Greek, means the "procreative power." We know now that the creative power spiritually is our tongue, our mouth, what we say. So this armor is to always put God's word in our mouth.

We are to have on the breastplate of righteousness. This means that we are always to be aware that we are forgiven and the Lord Himself is there in our hearts. We are in right standing with Him and must protect ourselves by reminding ourselves that the Lord has made us righteous and thereby silence the 'accuser of the brethren.' (Rev. 12:10)

Our feet are to be shod with the preparation of the gospel of peace. We looked at that word earlier. Peace means one or set at one again. We are to always be ready to walk as Jesus walked because He is in us wanting to walk to tell the good news of His love and sacrifice, and use God's power to help others.

Above all, we are to take the shield of faith – the protection from lies by our trust in the Word of God. Paul writes that by this shield we are able to "quench all the fiery darts of the wicked." Do you remember that James wrote *And the tongue is a fire, a world of iniquity: so is the tongue among our members, that it defileth the whole body, and settteth on fire the course of nature; and it is set on fire of hell.* (James 3:6) The enemy and the fallen angels that chose him over God are constantly wanting you to believe and speak other things than what God had said. That shield of faith is believing God's Word, no matter what things look like.

We are to take the helmet of salvation. That is like the breastplate of righteousness. Just as our hearts are to remember that God has made us righteous through Jesus Christ, our minds are always to be protected by the knowledge that He has saved us.

And we are to take the sword of the Spirit "which is the word of God." We are to defeat our enemies with the Word of God, believed in, fought for, and spoken out.

This list of armor begins and ends with the Word of God in our mouths. The devil hates that. He wants so much for his own words to be spoken out by you.

And we are to pray always in the Spirit with prayer and supplication for self and the world we live in and watch with all perseverance and supplication for all saints. That is a reminder that we are part of a Body and we must pray for one another – even those we don't know... "all saints."

Make HIM your life. He gave His life for you. Give yours for Him.

I will pray for your progress as well as my own. And I will pray for your loved ones who don't already, to come to know Jesus as their Lord, Love, and Life. Please pray for mine also.

# End Time Thoughts

Some time ago, the Lord told me to read all types of end time teachings and He would reveal Truth to me. I have studied Pre-Trib, Mid-Trib, and Post-Trib Rapture theories. I have studied Pre-Millennial, Post Millennial, and A-Millennial and non-rapture theories. I have come back to where I started in my own belief – that the Body of Christ will be taken out of this world before the seven years of the tribulation period before Jesus comes back to get rid of evil and set up His thousand year kingdom on the earth prior to the final judgement.

Jesus said of the catching away of the church *"But of that day and that hour knoweth no man, no, not the angels which are in heaven, neither the Son, but the Father. Take ye heed, watch and pray; for ye know not when the time is."* (Mark 13:32,33) That's an interesting statement because He definitely in several places tells them they should know the signs of the times.

Another thing I've studied in depth are the Feasts of the Lord, the Holy Convocations (and interestingly enough one of the definitions in Hebrew of convocation is rehearsal).

The seven feasts (which word has nothing to do with a meal but means appointed times) of the Lord listed in Leviticus 23 are Spring Feasts: Passover, Unleavened Bread, First Fruits, and Pentecost; and Fall Feasts: Trumpets, Atonement, and Tabernacles. The Lord fulfilled the Spring Feasts. He was crucified on Passover, He left our sins in hell during Unleavened Bread, He rose from the dead on First Fruits, and He poured out His Spirit on all flesh on Pentecost.

The Fall Feasts are not yet fulfilled. According to many Christians, including most Messianic Jews, the Feast of Trumpets (which is when they celebrate the creation of the world and humans were called to stop harvesting and come to the Temple to worship) is the time of the catching away of the church, Atonement is called the highest of holy days and believed to be when the

Jews realize that Jesus (Yeshua) really was the Messiah and repent, the Feast of Tabernacles will be when all God's children – Jews and Gentiles - will come together forever.

It could also be that there are three raptures: one before the tribulation of the Christians at that time; one at the middle of the tribulation of the 144 thousand from every tribe who realized when the Church was taken away that Jesus/Yeshua really was the Messiah and those they have converted; and one at the end, of those who turned to God during the time of the wrath. That could be why the Marriage Supper of the Lamb is shown right before Jesus comes back with all Believers instead of when the catching away of the church first happens. (Revelation 19).

But in all the studies of end times, one thing stood out to me and that is the reason I wrote this book. I believe that He is coming for a pure Bride, spotless and without blemish (Ephesians 5:25-27). It seems that the timing of the catching away of the Bride is up to you and me, the Church. God knows when it will happen because He knows everything but as we saw earlier *"His wife has made herself ready."* (Revelation 19:7,8) We are now in that process.

# Reflections

**LORD**

**Chapter One**
**Recognize Your Need for a Savior**

1. Do you believe that all humans are born with a sinful nature?
2. Have you recognized your need for a Savior?
3. In what areas do you miss the mark (sin)?
4. Some people say, "God and Jesus." Have you ever thought about their oneness, they are both God - Father and Son?

Did this chapter cause you to realize you need some goals in your life? What are they?

**Chapter Two**
**Receive Forgiveness and Rebirth**

1. Do you believe that Jesus (Yeshua/Savior) bore the punishment for all your sins on the cross?
2. Have you received the forgiveness He purchased for you?

3. Do you believe that God inspired people to write the Bible and that it shows His nature and will?

Did this chapter cause you to realize you need some goals in your life? What are they?

## Chapter Three
## Receive the Holy Spirit

1. Have you ever thought of the Holy Spirit as a force or a dove?
2. Have you experienced the Holy Spirit as a person?
3. Are you willing to receive more of the Holy Spirit in your life and actions?

Did this chapter cause you to realize you need some goals in your life? What are they?

## Chapter Four
## Gifts of the Spirit

1. Have you been immersed (baptized) in the Holy Spirit?
2. Do you think of a gift of the Spirit as belonging to you or a gift for someone else?
3. How have you experienced being a package,

or deliverer, of His gifts to someone else?

Did this chapter cause you to realize you need some goals in your life? What are they?

## Chapter Five
## Obey the Word and Communicate with Him

1. How often do you read, or listen to, the Bible?
2. Have you followed the law the way Jesus taught it?
3. Do you listen to the Lord and let Him teach you?

Did this chapter cause you to realize you need some goals in your life? What are they?

## LOVE

## Chapter Six
## Recognize and Reject Idols

1. What are the idols in your life?
2. Are you willing to get rid of them? All? Some? Which?
3. Are there any that you have gotten rid of in the past? If so, what are they?

Did this chapter cause you to realize you need some goals in your life? What are they?

## Chapter Seven
## Forgive Others and Self

1. Have you forgiven those who hurt you? If so list them.
2. Is there anyone you have not forgiven? If so list them. Are you willing to forgive them now?
3. Do you understand what forgiveness is in relation to Jesus on the cross?
4. Have you forgiven yourself? If not, are you willing to do so?

Did this chapter cause you to realize you need some goals in your life? What are they?

## Chapter Eight
## Worship Him in Song and Prayer

1. Where are you on St. Bernard of Clairvaux's love progression?
2. Do you like praise and worship music?
3. If so, which do you like best, if any?
4. Do you have a favorite hymn or song that

makes you feel close to the Lord?

Did this chapter cause you to realize you need some goals in your life? What are they?

## Chapter Nine
## Love Others

1. How do you serve others? List them?
2. As a child, did you have problems that damaged your self- image? If so, list them.
3. Has the Lord helped restore your self-respect? If so how?

Did this chapter cause you to realize you need some goals in your life? What are they?

## Chapter Ten
## Learn to Love Him Above All Else

1. Is Jesus the Love of your life yet? Be honest. If not, who is?
2. Do you know Him intimately?
3. If so, list some intimate times you've had with Him.
4. Have you ever seen His humor? Any other personal trait not taught to you by others?

Did this chapter cause you to realize you need some goals in your life? What are they?


**LIFE**

**Chapter Eleven**
**Remember You Are The Temple of The Holy Spirit**

>  1. Are you aware of being the Temple of the Holy Spirit? How often?
>  2. Are you aware of being the Body of Christ? (the physical vehicle of the Anointed One)
>  3. Looking back, can you see how He has changed you from one degree of being in His image to a greater degree?

Did this chapter cause you to realize you need some goals in your life? What are they?


**Chapter Twelve**
**Fruits of the Spirit**

1. Can you see that choosing to walk in the fruits of the Spirit is giving over parts of yourself to God.
2. Does it sometimes feel like crucifixion to your

flesh to choose to let His nature rule in your life?

3. Which fruit is the most difficult for you to walk in?

4. Which fruit comes the easiest to you?

Did this chapter cause you to realize you need some goals in your life? What are they?

## Chapter Thirteen
## Chosen

1. Do you realize that God chose you to be born and perfected before He created the world?

2. Do you see yourself adopted, born again, or both?

3. Does God know when you will become the perfect person He knows you as?

Did this chapter cause you to realize you need some goals in your life? What are they?

## Chapter Fourteen
## How the World Works

1. Does God creating this physical realm to work by quantum physics make any difference to you?

2. Do you realize the powerful impact your words have?
3. Do you want to be like those people in the Bible that the physical world did not hinder?

Did this chapter cause you to realize you need some goals in your life? What are they?

## Chapter Fifteen
## Stay in the Spirit

1. Which of the three persons of the Godhead (Trinity) do you feel the closest to?
2. Are you aware that you have been assigned the character of the Lord Jesus Christ?
3. Do you realize that God Himself is your protection from your enemy, the devil?

Did this chapter cause you to realize you need some goals in your life? What are they?

## End Time Thoughts

What are your beliefs about end times? Why do you believe that way?

# Acknowledgements

First of all, I want to thank our Lord Jesus for giving me this message. Then His daughter and mine, Virginia Patrick Smith, without whom I would never have had any of my Christian books published. Thank you to Nick Delliskave for putting the cover together. Thank you to my husband Gary Barkman who is always supportive of anything I do for the Lord, no matter how much time it takes.

I'm grateful to my other two Christian daughters, Susie Patrick Smith and Beth Waits Marlowe for their continuing encouragement. I'm grateful to all who have loved my books and told me so, especially Jacque Lea, Patty Parker, Betsy Banks, and Jackie Lunsford. Thank you to my Church family and my Bible study groups, the Voice of Joy annual seminar attendees and annual Mikvah retreat participants. Without their encouragement and love, I would probably have given up ministry long ago.

And I have a special thank you to Pastor David Moore who heard me teach this message at a workshop in Springfield, Ill at the national Aldersgate Renewal Ministries Conference in 2019 and said afterwards, "You need to be teaching this everywhere!" That is the reason I started putting the message into book form.

# Books by Amy Barkman

## Christian Adult Fiction
Tapestry Court Series:
Murder at Tapestry Court
Danger at Tapestry Court

Victims
To Love Again

## Middle Grade Fiction
Fun To Be One Club Christian Series:
Which Witch?
Chaos at Camp?

Kentucky Adventures (Historical Fiction)

## Christian Non-Fiction
Everyday Spiritual Warfare
The Progression of Perfection